To Gayle – thank you, sweetheart.

Table of Contents

In Your Wildest ...

Preface

Culture earthquake - It's hard to fully understand the impulsive, erratic nature of events as they unfolded during the mid to late 'Sixties. History was in a mood: defy the norm and break out; throw off restraints, innovate, rebel, add color; disregard mores and traditions. Those of us caught in its tantrum can remember with great vividness what happened; events unfolded so quickly, so dramatically, so forcefully and in some cases, so traumatically - like the child who grows up with an alcoholic father or a bi-polar mother. You might not remember what you got for your seventh Christmas but you sure as hell remember which hospital Dad was in that Christmas and how he got there. Living at the whims of someone's moods does that; and history was definitely having its mood and dishing out its share of trauma.

The great Shudder. In the desert southwest along the Rio Grande Valley, pecan farmers harvest ripe pecans using a tree shaker. It's a large four-wheeled vehicle that looks like a souped-up Humvee with hydraulic pincers extending off of its front that grab the trunk of the pecan tree and shake it. Ripe pecans fall to the ground and are gathered by a "sweeper." When history shook, it made its impact ... and things fell out of the branches.

In the fallout came a happening or movement or something that no one saw coming – triggered by the Shudder, it affected tens of millions of people worldwide.

New ideas were asserting themselves and messing with people all the way from Greenwich Village, to Max Yasgur's farm in New York, to muddy fields near Kickapoo Creek, IL to Old Town, Chicago to San Francisco's Haight – Ashbury, London, Liverpool and Amsterdam. It didn't matter where you lived, what you believed, how you'd been raised, what war you'd fought in, what values you'd been raised with or what religion you espoused – just shake it up, baby.

Bob Dylan remembered: "People today are still living off the table scraps of the 'Sixties. They are still being passed around - the music and the ideas."[1] My kids talk about some of those ideas even today. (Amie read Jack Kerouac's "On the Road" before I did.) The 'Sixties' cries for social justice, which, I believe, helped a lot of people and gave birth to a newer, fresher collective sensitivity in our culture on how disenfranchised people should be treated – those cries resonate with not just our kids but with millions of others their age. I love that about the 'Sixties.

---

[1] "Bob Dylan." BrainyQuote.com. Xplore Inc, 2012. 16 November 2012
http://www.brainyquote.com/quotes/quotes/b/bobdylan154490.html

June 21, 1971 – the cover story for Time Magazine entitled The Jesus Revolution. Here's how the article began:

WANTED
JESUS CHRIST
ALIAS: THE MESSIAH, THE SON OF GOD,
KING OF KINGS, LORD OF LORDS,
PRINCE OF PEACE, ETC.
Notorious leader of an underground
liberation movement

Wanted for the following charges:

Practicing medicine, winemaking and food
distribution without a license

Interfering with businessmen in the temple

Associating with known criminals, radicals,
subversives, prostitutes and street people

Claiming to have the authority to make
people into God's children

APPEARANCE: Typical hippie type—long
hair, beard, robe, sandals

Hangs around slum areas, few rich friends,
often sneaks out into the desert

BEWARE: This man is extremely dangerous. His insidiously inflammatory message is particularly dangerous to young people who haven't been taught to ignore him yet. He changes men and claims to set them free.

WARNING: HE IS STILL AT LARGE!

This was a quote from a poster that this Time magazine journalist had found in "a Christian underground newspaper." Imagine that – in the midst of the Shudder, a bit of Christianity shook loose and found some fertile soil in the hearts and minds of the very people it was shaking! And what a group: hippies, drug addicts, street dwellers, highway wanderers, commune-dwelling seekers, oriental and occidental religionists, poets, musicians, prostitutes, runaways, mental cases, disillusioned church members. And the "underground" part of the Christian underground newspaper? Not for long. Picture the zombie's hand breaking through the damp, fetid soil – the monster we thought was long dead.

That was 1971 but things were already happening – from L.A. to Chicago to New York City to Miami; from cities to burgs to farm communities and suburbs – history's tantrum had a Hitchhiker making a whole lot of history of his own, and he wasn't about to keep it underground.

Introduction

"A ship in harbor is safe - but that is not what ships are for." ~ John A. Shedd, Salt from My Attic

"You'll always miss 100% of the shots you don't take." ~ Wayne Gretzky

I have a friend, Mark Gungor, who lives in Green Bay, WI and is senior pastor at Celebration Church and an internationally known relationships speaker. He and his wife, Debbie, traveled with Gayle and me for several years in the seventies and shared in many of our experiences. Once Mark called me and told me he'd been trying to tell some of our stories to staff and members at his church (now our church). He described how blank stares gave way to uncertain smiles and then, "Okay, Mark. Whatever you say!" (Eyes rolling back) He's already had to call me for backup.

Early Lutherans were quoted as saying, "Faith is a perturbing thing." I mention this because, as you read these stories and vignettes, your eyebrows may rise slightly, your head may shake from side to side in periodic disbelief, and you may smile and think, "He's making this up." So let's see if you believe it. I loved Dave Barry's newspaper columns and his nervous assurance to us when he felt a story coming on that no sane person would ordinarily believe, "I am not making this up!" This is like that - not in your wildest imagination.

Our experiences ran the gamut: bizarre circumstances and bizarre people, healings, demons, manifestations, miraculous provision and the dead being raised. Yes, – dead people rising up! I discovered something wonderful about miracles through all of that: it doesn't matter whether people believe you when you tell the story. All that matters is that that person for whom the miracle was performed experienced the compassion of God in that moment. That's all there is to it. He experienced it. He lived it. He became the recipient of a gracelet when God opened, for one indescribable moment, the gateway of heaven and overshadowed that one precious individual with miracle and mercy.

Put enough of those stories and individuals together and you'll have what the physician, Luke, wrote: The Book Acts, or, as others have called it, the book of Facts. Had I not seen these things with my own eyes, it would have remained somebody else's book; somebody else's facts, but now it's my book, too. Be honest, if you could see just one supernatural miracle; one single "science fiction" transformed into "non-fiction," before your own eyes, wouldn't that be beyond awesome? You have to be intellectually honest to say "yes" to that. What if you could beam up? What if Spock or ET could simply touch you and you'd heal? What if you could

be Spock or ET or Wolverine or Yoda? 'Fess up –
you know you'd dig it!

Truth be told, we just happened to be in the vicinity
when God decided to make life more interesting,
and in come cases, where fiction transformed into
non-fiction, and these are some of our stories.

There are hundreds of you who were close by when
these things happened, so I have to put a qualifier in
here. This is how it looked through my eyes. I'm
certain much of it looked different through yours.
But this mini-history is for you because you went
through it; you saw it and experienced it. You
sacrificed and suffered and displayed super-human
courage and humility.

Most of us are grandparents now! Be sure to tell
your stories to your grandkids. They may not
believe you but you can be dead honest: you were
there; you saw it with your own eyes; there's
nothing to apologize for; you are NOT making this
up.

This is my book but our journey, "our" referring to
my wife, our kids and our traveling companions
over a decade-long odyssey. To chronicle what we
saw is the reason I'm writing; not what we learned,
but what we saw. Everyone on this journey learned
different things, but we all saw pretty much the
same things. Someone said that a man with an
experience is never at the mercy of a man with an
argument. To enter into debate over what hundreds

of us experienced would be a waste of time. You just had to be there.

We believe God inspired and instigated this amazing decade. It deserves a complete story, and this is my attempt. Add to this hundreds and thousands of other stories from our group and there would be no book big enough to hold it all. The apostle wrote:

"Jesus did many other things as well. If every one of them were written down, I suppose that even the whole world would not have room for the books that would be written." - John 21:25

I didn't understand that verse when I first read it, but I'm starting to now. This book is an extremely abridged account of God touching the lives of several hundred of my fellow witnesses. Multiply that into the hundreds of millions in the constellation of history and the unseen church, each person with his own astonishing story, and there it is: the chronicles no book could ever contain.

John said, "Jesus did many other things." Apparently it was what He did, what others experienced when He acted, that made the bigger impression. The parables and teachings of Jesus are short and, in most cases, unaccompanied by context or embellishment. What we read in the four gospels was pretty much all that could be remembered and recorded. But John doesn't point to the Words as much as the Deeds. We seem to remember deeds.

"The people were all so amazed that they asked each other, "What is this? A new teaching – and with authority! He even gives orders to evil spirits and they obey him." - Mark 1:27

His actions were so breathtaking, they were left without words; only with questions: "What is this, a new teaching?" – Really? As if a teaching could raise the dead or drive out demons? They were confused. At a time when we are immersed in a culture of words and knowledge, it's refreshing to know that there are people out there actually doing things. Doing something makes a much better book than talking about doing something. Do it first, then write about it. I think that makes sense. So we did, we experienced, we stepped out and we took the risks ... and we saw things beyond our wildest collective imaginations. This is our story. Happy reading.

Chapter One
Birthing Giants

Some people are just more open to the spiritual, I think. Not sure why. Maybe it's hard-wired from birth; maybe what happens early in life affects them and an unconscious search for escape or for something better begins. John the Baptist did somersaults in the womb when he first heard Jesus' mother Mary. Bet your kid didn't do that. And imagine young John walking into the house one day, the boy whom you knew was called to great things, chewing on locusts:

"Mom, what's a brood of vipers? I just had a run-in with some brats down at school and it just came out of my mouth."

Rebekah's twin babies "jostled each other within her, and she said, 'Why is this happening to me?'"; and Jacob held onto Esau's heel while they descended through the birth canal: "No, this isn't right. I'm supposed to be first!"

Jacob was right: Later God said, "I have loved Jacob, but Esau have I hated." Esau – the embodiment of Murphy's Law.

That's what I mean; John doing somersaults, Jacob and Esau jostling. (Apparently I did my share of leaping in the womb, too, because I was born with a left hip completely out of socket) – hardwired for action; let 'er rip! "Why am I still in here?" They couldn't wait to be born - the call, the mission, the divine urge to get on with things was already there motivating, energizing, pushing. Elizabeth and Rebekah were birthing babies, titans really, who were themselves already in their own type of birthing agonies waiting to be loosed from their physical confines so that their march toward destiny could begin.

Where does that sense of destiny come from? How does a divine, in utero urge grab hold of a person like that, like a John the Baptist or a Jacob?

It happens differently for different people – Samuel was around twelve when he first heard God speak, but put yourself in his shoes – a 12-year-old and God says to you: "See, I am about to do something in Israel that will make the ears of everyone who hears of it tingle." And then the message of doom on Eli's household – the curse of God on a whole family! That gets a twelve-year-old PG-13 rating in my book, but apparently God was ok with it.

"Samuel, I'm going to tell you first. Now be a good boy and convey that to Eli," - Samuel's twelve-year-old ears doing their own share of the tingle trot.

Here's a comparable scenario: you grow up a good Catholic and at twelve you go through your catechism and on a special spring Sunday morning you're just about ready to go forward for the priest's blessing and confirmation and then an audible voice in your ear: "The guilt of the priest's household will never be forgiven." Great fun.

David was about the same age when Samuel, now an old man, called him out; Jesus taught the priests in Jerusalem's temple at twelve. Twelve-year-old kids just don't do things like that. Babies don't do somersaults or jostle each other for first dibs out. But there it is – history's confirmation to us that some people connect with God very early; some people are sensitive to God in a way most never understand. He speaks when, how and to whom He wills.

And then there are the broken ones – people who grow up in impossible situations: abused, neglected, terrorized. People who don't hear the voice of God at twelve, they hear the dad raging in the basement; they come home to the mother nodding off in a drug stupor. Drug counselors, school counselors, pediatric therapists, psychiatrists, social workers and law enforcement officers become the only adults they really ever interact with. "Behold, my default family."

The broken ones – "And why do you think you were jostling in the womb, Jimmy?"

"Easy, I was partying with Mom inside my pickled placenta."

My guess is that there are more broken ones than Jacobs or Samuels or John the Baptists. I was among them. But even the broken ones, at times, are able to catch the Voice, even in the midst of their hell storm, and they respond and things change.

Dad first went to the hospital when I was in seventh grade. It was Christmas week and this awful argument – yelling and things falling over upstairs, thuds coming through the ceiling; sounds like the far-off thunder of an approaching storm – "Ed, stop that right now!" I was in disbelief. Mom came downstairs, got on the phone to the neighbors and we went there. We were returned home several hours later – Mom and Grandpa sitting in the living room explaining to my sister and me that Dad had to go to the hospital; that he was very sad and needed help – the beginning of sorrows.

We learned a lot about bi-polar disorder over the ensuing years, how it doesn't work well with alcoholism, how a person suffering under this kind of torment is further tormented when he wakes up in the hospital and is told that he just tore his house apart, kicked his 12-year-old son, tried pulling the plumbing out of the wall in the basement, threatened bodily harm to his wife and "Ed, you really need to take your meds, even when you don't think you need them." People who were your friends, aren't anymore; families who used to invite you over, don't anymore; and a family unit disintegrates into 3 people living in a house with a ticking time bomb.

For me, the father I should have loved and respected as I grew into adulthood became the anti-father; the one who terrorized me and drove me into hiding. David and Samuel were called of God at twelve; in my twelfth year, I was introduced into chaos and trauma at the hands of the one person who was supposed to provide stability and safety. Good times.

So, some are born with a spiritual calling and some aren't. As with Samuel, God gets their ear early and off they go. But for most people, and that's why I use myself as an example, there seems to be a process that goes on inside and outside until the Voice can be heard and responded to. That happens; but not always: sometimes the early abuse and trauma produces anything but tenderness toward God.

> Adolph Hitler's father gave him regular beatings. He was authoritarian, selfish and hard; ... Josef Stalin's father was the same, giving him repeated, undeserved beatings after he had finished with Stalin's mother; and ... Mao Zedong's father was also harsh and described as a family tyrant and inspired a rebellious spirit in his son which later became the foundation for the communist movement in China. Yes, three of the past century's worst tyrants were themselves tyrannized at home by their fathers ... Children learn best by example, and they always tend to follow the example set at home or the lack of example.

Seventy percent of juvenile felons in the U.S. have no fathers. [2]

I'll never know how close I came to a Stalin-type hopelessness, but an indicator of a better future took place in 1967, my junior year: we had a guest speaker for a mandatory assembly at school. We were in the gym because the assembly auditorium couldn't hold all of us. He was from New York City (Pastor John Gimenez) and his platform was anti-drug awareness, but 15 minutes into his talk we all knew there was something really different about this guy.

His was the story of a heroin addict on a $300/day habit (that's three hundred 1960 dollars); stealing, lying, robbing, anything to get that day's fix and then the invitation into a tiny church in the Bronx where he joined other addicts and found freedom from heroin. The power in his story hit home, like something got hold of my gut, when he mentioned the fact that it was prayer and faith that brought him his deliverance; this, in a public high school assembly! He had his books for sale; I bought one, asked him to sign it and spent the next week reading it from cover to cover - my first introduction to what the power of God could do in a person's life even when that person had given up hope.

---

[2] *Faith of the Fatherless, The Psychology of Atheism,* Paul Vitz, copyright 2002

Chapter Two
Even the Stoned Cry Out!

Some of the Pharisees in the crowd said to Jesus, "Teacher, rebuke your disciples!"

"I tell you," he replied, "if they keep quiet, the stones will cry out ..." or in our case, "the stoned will cry out."

My sister, Janie, experienced God before I did. She was at church youth group one night. They were praying and holding hands and all of a sudden God was there. She called me later on the phone and told me about it. Her voice was filled with wonder, tinged with a little fear, and I was filled with immediate skepticism. "We'll see," I said to myself. It was 1969.

I first picked up a guitar in 7th grade. So did a lot of kids in those days. The Beatles were on the radio. No one had ever heard anything like it and it was guitar-driven music and simple to the ear. That's why a lot of kids were picking up guitars. My first songbook was music to the "Hard Day's Night" album; and then seventh grade warped into 1967.

A lot was happening – I'd become more integrated into my musical tribe and we were busy playing festivals, taverns, college campuses, frat parties and concerts. The most important thing for a teenager is to be a part of a group. He is working his way out from under the umbrella of parental authority and becomes preoccupied with finding a self-identity. This is tricky given the fact that the 16-year-old is still, in many ways, a child ("I've gotta be me, whatever that is.") and not in any way prepared for the real world. But he doesn't know that. And so he's okay expressing his independence, a conditional independence, a dependent independence, based on which group he identifies with other than his parents. Take your pick: jocks, geeks, Goths, druggies, cheerleaders, cheerleader groupies, brainiacs ... musicians!

When you live in a home inhabited by a time bomb (my bi-polar father) and you're deciding which group is going to give you your new identity as an emerging adult, the choice is much easier to make – you go with whatever can give the quickest escape from reality and away from your crazy father. Music for me.

In the two years leading up to my departure for college there were multiple music opportunities with a potpourri of musicians and music styles: blues, rock, jazz in a very compressed period of time - my most memorable years in music covering songs from Frank Zappa to Eric Clapton to Jimi Hendrix to Blood, Sweat and Tears to the Beatles to The Doors.

High school graduation in 1969 led to enrollment at Illinois State with the summer leading up to that filled with amazing music experiences. Moving into my dorm room was a bit of a downer. I was the only guy on my floor and maybe the whole dormitory with long hair AND a guitar. Classes were intense and intimidating. Around Christmas I received a phone call from a "Dave" who was in a band called Gideon's Bible, and they were looking for a guitar player. I auditioned, joined the band and we were in the recording studio within a few weeks. I made it into my second freshman semester at Illinois State and dropped out in order to go full time with the band; moved into a house with the other band members just off campus, and my parents all but disowned me when they discovered that I'd dropped out of college.

I'm sure it really did look like I'd lost my mind. My father was furious; so was my mother, but probably for a different reason. She knew what this would precipitate at home with him and it wouldn't be pretty. Dads have dreams for their kids – they hope that their son or daughter will grow up to be greater, better, more successful, better off than Dad. It contributes to a father's pride and self-esteem: "I must have done something right. He turned out way better than me." For my Dad and many dads that usually meant a college degree. If the child doesn't measure up, that is also a reflection on the father (the father imagines) and it reduces him in the eyes of his peers. I may as well have spit in his eye – he was that angry (and probably embarrassed).

The band prospered. It was only weeks since we had all withdrawn from college and pledged ourselves to nothing less than absolute success in an industry that promised exactly nothing. They were heady days, but not much thought was going into what might happen if IT didn't happen – there was no plan B. Shortly after our new recording was out, we moved from Bloomington, Illinois and our college surroundings to Indianapolis, the home of our band's manager. Everything went into "Tar Baby," our eighteen-foot, 1957 Ford truck painted completely black, stem to stern.

We were facing a lawsuit threat from Gideon's International for trademark infringement due to the name of the band, so we went from Gideon's Bible to "e" (e for ecology, eternity, energy, ESP, Eden ... add esoteric to that list because we all took a certain pride in being the next unique thing to come along – "Yes, you're special, just like everyone else.")

Indianapolis: living in a house with five other musicians, bridges burned and visions of bright lights and big cities. In a very short period of time "e" had opened for Janis Joplin, Ted Nugent, Country Joe McDonald, The Flock and Richie Havens. I'd already rubbed shoulders and played in bands with local buddies from the Peoria area: Mike Sommerville (Head East); Dan Fogelberg (Dan Fogelberg); Gary Richrath (REO Speedwagon); Ron Stockert (Rufus) where we opened for the likes of The Guess Who and Uriah Heep. Like I said, these were heady days for rock 'n roll musicians! My personal Shudder, as I described earlier, was about to begin.

Within four weeks of my arrival in Indy, we were on stage opening for Janis Joplin.

It was also during those summer months that we all agreed that the dope smoking, pill-popping days were over. We discovered transcendental meditation; we became vegetarians; we pledged ourselves to a complete detoxification of our strung out bodies and minds and knew it was the right thing to do.

There was good reason: one of the guys in the band had a nasty LSD flashback. He was seeing things and ended up in a psyche ward after his brain decided it had taken one too many acid baths. Our house ended up with fist-sized holes in the walls and doors torn off hinges as he came unhinged. He spent the next two days in a straight jacket. I can't remember being that scared - ever. And that's why we decided that detox was a good thing.

About the same time as the group detox was in progress, we met hippies from California, converts to the "you've-got-to-experience-this" gang, which in those days meant pushy Christian people who had, in our opinion, gone over to the bad side of religion. They invited us to a prayer meeting, similar to the one my sister had attended years before, where we were sure we would be surrounded by similar "you've-got-to-experience-this" kinds of people.

Actually they invited David, our drummer, to the prayer meetings along with his girlfriend, Lynn. The rest of us were in hiding or conveniently indisposed. David, being the open-minded mystic that he was, attended their meeting and came home wide-eyed, lowered his head, shook it and, after a long exhale, said, "Man, you really need to check this out, guys. These people are speaking in tongues (remember the tongues of fire that appeared over the heads of the disciples and what happened after?), having visions, reading the Bible and saying that all that Bible stuff is still for today."

And then he and Lynn went again and came home at a loss for words: "They cast a demon out of this guy tonight! It was a total freak-out!"

And in my mind I was going, "Why can't we just eat vegetables and meditate and be left alone?" It was too much, too fast and something inside me rose up, determined that I would not yield to these new ideas.

Chapter Three
Hippies in Church

Well, the trees are rustlin' in the woods,
Things are fallin' off the shelves.
- Bob Dylan

We'd all been living hand to mouth that summer, existing on what little income there was from our side jobs. David signed up to sell family Bibles door to door (go figure). We had CARTONS full of them out in the garage. They ended up not selling so well, David looking the way he did and all – a six foot six man with long, somewhat frizzy hair, long beard and wild eyes dressed in torn blue jeans and beat up gym shoes walks up to your door with a family Bible and asks if he can come in and show you why you need this Bible on your coffee table – and you say ... what do you say, exactly?

"Please come in, I've just been waiting for someone like you to come to my door peddling, you know, family Bibles like this."

It just wasn't meant to be. But at least David had the biggest, whitest Bible anyone had ever seen when he showed up at that first Bible meeting where people spoke in tongues and demons were being cast out. If I'd been a demon and seen David's Bible, I also would have left voluntarily or peed my demon pants ... or both.

So after the second or third night's meeting, David returned home with his family Bible and his stories, bubbling with excitement about what he'd seen and experienced at these meetings. The rest of us were skeptical and had nowhere near the spiritual hunger David had, so we just stayed home. But that third night, when he walked in, he asked me if I'd be open to just sitting down at the kitchen table with him so he could read to me some of the things they'd been hearing at the Bible study, and I said, "Well, okay;" because I didn't want to be a jerk about it and what harm could it do. And the first night David read the entire book of Revelations to me, all twenty-two chapters, and I have to admit, it was so intriguing I only remember taking one potty break.

At the end of Revelations, David looked up and said simply, "The guys at the meeting tonight said that what I just read to you is about to happen soon; that Jesus is coming and that people need to get ready."

"Hmm," I said, not knowing what else to say; and went to bed.

After night number four, David came home and read all five chapters of John's first epistle (mercifully shorter) as we sat again at the kitchen table at midnight near 38th Street and Meridian in Indianapolis and I almost started crying. The first epistle of John was a letter written at large by, you guessed it, to the churches at large in his day with a simple theme – "God is love, he loves us, and therefore we ought to love one another." The reason

I almost cried was because those five short chapters embodied every other-worldly, flower-power, esoteric value that we'd been searching for and trying to capture in our mystical, musical experience. We'd read everything from the Upanishads to Jonathan Seagull to Gibran's The Prophet to the Koran. We'd talked and sung and philosophized at length about the power of love, but why hadn't anyone ever read these Bible verses to us? It was all there – right there! As David read this to me, I realized – "Man (we said "man" a lot, not "dude"), we don't have to look anywhere else if this stuff is really true."

The angel of the Lord showed up one night and told Mary that she would soon conceive a baby through the miraculous intervention of the Holy Spirit and that he would be the Savior of the world. The Bible says she kept these things to herself and pondered them in her heart. That's kind of what I felt like after that night keeping company with David and John's first epistle. I pondered; I wondered; I waited to see what might happen next.

Life had been depressing during the previous months. I'd been lonely, desperate and feeling lost, especially feeling guilt at quitting college to pursue this music career to the displeasure of my parents; and now living in Indianapolis with no job, no music career and, worst of all, no food! All of the elbow rubbing we'd done with all of the stars and personalities the previous year had yielded exactly zero money and exactly no music career resulting in exactly zero food. Well, we did have butterscotch syrup, a head of cauliflower and some popcorn oil that we actually did manufacture into a meal of sorts: cauliflower, fried in popcorn oil smothered in butterscotch syrup. And there's nothing like a fried-cauliflower-with-butterscotch-syrup dinner to prepare you for the possibility that maybe there's something better out there.

And there was – a potluck to be specific; a down-home, pot-roast-and-potato-filled potluck with tons of other goodies. "Pot luck" for hippies – how ironic - "We scored!" (I digress.) Yes, God used a potluck to draw us in a little closer: "Come here, little fella; all you have to do is edge this way and you can have dinner!" And we gladly accepted the invitation to the potluck sponsored by the very people David had been going to see the previous week – the ones speaking in tongues and casting out demons. Isn't it amazing how something as simple as food can break down just about any barriers we put up? All five of us in the band, the very incarnation of starving musicians, were invited to this banquet with one caveat: would we consider staying afterward for a short Bible study?

So ... we stayed ... and indeed, they did have a prayer meeting/Bible study right after dinner. We did not go for the prayer nor did we go for the Bible study. The food was delicious to an empty stomach and a long-deprived palate, and the church people were – different. I can't imagine how we appeared to them. The "preacher" got up after the meal, invited us into the living room of the home, the people sang and prayed and lifted their hands, and then he spoke.

He was not a professionally-trained pastor. He ran a lathe at the local Allis Chalmers plant in Speedway (a west-side suburb of Indianapolis). But when he spoke, he glowed. Brother Bud Earle actually glowed with something beatific, something I had never seen. He never looked at us. When he spoke, he was looking somewhere else – over our heads – like he was seeing something very beautiful and describing it to us.

The deacon, Stephen, preached in Jerusalem to members of the Sanhedrin; here's what Acts 6:15 says about that: "All who were sitting in the Sanhedrin looked intently at Stephen, and they saw that his face was like the face of an angel." That's what Bud looked like. I had never seen a face like that. And when he'd finished, we (the five members of the "e band") were on our knees, crying, asking God if there might be some way He could forgive our wretched lives and make us into something He could use.

All five of us met Christ that night. There, in a tiny home, in Speedway, on the floor - an entire rock band in one fell swoop; bowing, not to an audience, but to a King; not acknowledging applause but acknowledging our infinite number of sins. The stoned cried out. What a sight we must have been to heaven. And I can hear the posse of angels assigned to us – "Great, now what?"

Chapter Four
Elfriede

Elfriede was there that night in Speedway. It was her house where we met. She was the strangest lady - about five foot two and looked like Mrs. Santa Claus. She even sounded like Mrs. Santa Claus. Elfriede had the most beautiful smile, which erupted whenever she saw us. Her eyes twinkled mischievously as if she were always planning some surprise. We five were "her boys."

She was German and had this lilting, flowing accent, like Mrs. Claus would have had. She escaped Nazi Germany during the War after almost having been murdered on a German train by some out-of-control Gestapo who happened onto the train looking for Jews and decided to spray the place with machine gun fire for no apparent reason. After arriving in the U.S., she married and had kids. The family left home as did the husband, and she was left alone in Indianapolis with nothing – except terminal cancer.

The doctors sent her home from the hospital to die even though there was no one to care for her. One day, she had had enough and resolved not to let the cancer take her. She went into the kitchen, turned on the gas in the oven and stuck her head inside.

And she told us, her voice cracking and her eyes tearing up with deep emotion, "As I schtuck my head in ze oven, somevun said my name. At first I didn't listen, but he said it again, only a little louder so I vouldn't mistake it for a bad dream or zumzing. I turned from ze oven, looked up, and Yaysus was schtanding zer. He reached out and touched my head and told me ' go back to bed.' I voke up ze next morning, passed zumzing in ze toilet that was foul smelling and black and zen I vent to ze doctor."

They examined Elfriede and found not a trace of the cancer.

"And I have lovt Him and servt Him ever since," she beamed. "And I vill pray for you boys every day, and I vill be zhere for you. Ze zame vonderful Yaysus who touched me has touched you, and God has called you boys to bring His message to your generation troo your music." And we did, and she did.

Chapter Five
Jesus Freaks

We were the number one local band in Indy. Everyone knew us. We were famous to some and becoming more so; notorious to others, particularly parents. One of us sold drugs and womanized; I drank and womanized; another took LSD. He's the one who ended up in the psych ward.

Our keyboardist had been in various nightclub bands and our bass player was a hippie in the south Florida Coconut Grove scene. What a bunch. So when the word started spreading around town that we were "different" now, people wanted to know more. How different were they? We started writing new words to new songs that had a lot to do with our new faith. We were "contemporary Christian artists" before there was such a thing, at least in the Midwest. So we were in uncharted waters.

Our opening engagement as Christian artists was at the Green Onion on the east side of Indianapolis. The place was packed, we had been signed by the owner for two weeks, the booze flowed freely, the people were ready to party, and we started singing ... about Jesus. During our breaks between sets, because we didn't know better, we sat down with the patrons and showed them Christian literature, tracts, street newspapers from the L.A. Jesus freak scene – anything we could get our hands on. People would break down crying at their tables as they spoke with us. What else are you going to do when you've just spent $40 on drinks with your date and this happens? Tears of shear joy. Seriously, others willingly and openly prayed with us for Christ to become real in their lives.

Brother Bud, his wife, Eileen, and Elfriede were in attendance - kind of - sitting nervously in the back nursing their ice water and praying like crazy for us and probably for themselves. We were oblivious to the problem. Didn't Christians always give witness in settings like this? Wasn't it normal to pray for drunks over their cocktails? Brother Bud would manage a smile and say "Thank you, Jesus." They really were proud of us. And for us there was no problem – at least for the first week of our two-week contract.

Paul, the apostle, preached in the city of Philippi and was joined one day by a girl who was possessed by a spirit of divination. She was a slave and evidently brought her owners a lot of money by her supernatural ability to tell and sell the future. Acts 16:16 says "she earned a great deal of money for her owners." Paul could see the spirit in her and cast it out, which was good and bad – good that she was free, bad that her owners could no longer pimp her out. And they were really pissed and had Paul and his companion, Silas, dragged before the magistrates and thrown in jail. We were not thrown in jail but that following Saturday night, the owner of the Green Onion sat us down and terminated our

contract. He'd lost one thousand 1970-type dollars
in liquor sales that week.

The "E" House

We all lived in a former dental office near 38th and
Meridian in Indianapolis. Each of our bedrooms
had been converted from treatment rooms
previously used for the poor souls under the drill.
There were five of us plus our road manager living
there. The living room was for rehearsals and Bible
studies. We also had a big driveway and two-car
garage so after rehearsals in the morning we'd head
out to the driveway for basketball – three on three.
We were pretty good; even joined an intramural
league.

After the word spread around town that "E Band"
had found Jesus, kids started dropping by with
problems, needing to talk. There were high
schoolers strung out on marijuana or speed or LSD.
They were dealing with all sorts of sexual issues.
Some had been involved a little too deeply in
witchcraft and now couldn't sleep at night. We even
had a former satanic priestess who kept coming by.
She wanted to know Christ, but every time I prayed
with her, a demon would manifest, and she would
begin cursing me. Once she said it told her to kill
me.

She called one night asking if I'd come over to pray with her and her baby boy. She said she had awakened in the night and her ex-husband, a satanic high-priest, had "manifested" over her baby's crib and was threatening to kill the baby unless she agreed to come back to him and re-enter satanic worship. I am not making this up.

"Can you just come over and pray over my room and over the crib," Gerry asked. This creeped me out, but I went anyway. We entered the room, I prayed, rebuking the devil without a clue as to what I was doing.

All of a sudden I heard a hoarse whisper, "Joe, look!" And I turned to see the closet door slowly opening. I'd had enough; it was the middle of the night, I'd been awakened from a dead sleep – I got angry and charged into the closet and told whoever it was in there to get out. And then – peace; she was able to sleep peacefully that night. Gerry walked with Christ for a while, but the drugs, which had been her life, eventually drew her away - unbelievable problems and unbelievable spiritual hunger. Doing Christianity in those days was like entering a war zone: great victories with many casualties and much collateral damage. One couple that had found Christ and had been delivered from drug addiction claimed that God spoke to them one night to sacrifice their newborn baby like God had commanded Abraham to do with his son, Isaac. They are both still in prison.

We didn't know much more than the kids did, but we let them come to the house anyway. We had just taken down the pictures of our own gurus from the walls. (Jesus, of course, was right up there with the Maharishi.) Brother Bud, Eileen and Elfriede would sneak into the room where we'd hung the pictures of our spiritual heroes and pray that we'd figure it out, and we did without them having to speak one condemning word.

"Taking kids in" soon turned into a regular Tuesday night Bible study. There was never enough room. They flocked to the Bible study and Brother Earle, Eileen and sister Elfriede were in their prime. And the kids loved them. And hundreds came to know Christ. The "e band" played in any venue that would have us and word would spread and the kids would show up.

Curtis, a small, quiet African-American man came to every one of our Bible studies. He prayed for me often. By that time Jim Jones had begun a branch of his People's Temple in Indianapolis and many spiritually hungry folks began attending, drawn by his charismatic personality and spiritual fervor. Of course what they didn't know was that Jones had been a lifelong Marxist (born in 1931 in, of all places, Clown, Indiana) and was using his form of religion to draw people out of religion, the "opiate of the masses," so they would eventually see the light and help build a new Marxist social order here in the U.S.

We sensed there was something wrong there and never went. That seemed to be the year of the cults for Indianapolis. Moses David Berg's The Children of God and Victor Paul Wierwille's The Way International both swept through town and feasted off of the young people who had exercised faith in Christ at our concerts or in our Bible studies. We lost many of the young ones to those groups, and a good percentage of them fell away from their faith as a result. Curtis told me one night that he'd decided to start attending Jim Jones' church. He really sang his praises and tried convincing us to attend with him, but we declined. That was the last time we saw Curtis, and I always wondered if he'd ended up in Guyana, drinking the cyanide-laced Flavor-Aid.

We played at one of the Midwest's first Jesus festivals in Evansville, Indiana and headlined with a rising star from the West Coast named Larry Norman, the father of contemporary Christian music. Larry was the most gentle, gracious person, and we had a great time with him. From the Evansville festival, word got around about e band and where we were from and soon we were playing all over. A chaplain for the Cook County jail named Ron Rendleman took us under his wing and began booking us in every Chicago-area high school he could find. It was a great time – anti-drug concerts in school auditoriums by day followed by Jesus concerts in the same auditoriums at night (so as not to violate church/state separation - hehe). Hundreds of kids would come to Christ during these rally/concerts. Their hunger for a real God and a real experience with a real God was palpable and miraculous.

Chapter Six
Our First Revival at 70 Degrees Below Zero

We'd run into them from time to time when the band played in the Chicago area. They were "The Sheep," and we were still " e." They looked like we did and played the same kind of music we did, but there was something about them that always seemed to make me uneasy. "The Sheep" were part of a commune of a hundred plus Jesus freaks (more freak than Jesus) living in downtown Milwaukee. They had left literally everything to serve God and spent their days on the streets talking to people about the gospel. "The Sheep" were merely a musical extension of their ministry and not by any means an entity unto themselves. It was all one big, happy, loony family.

God told them to go to Duluth, Minnesota to preach there in early winter, 1971. He didn't say anything else; just that they were to go: Duluth, Minnesota – January – 86.1 inches of snowfall per year with average recorded snowfalls in May and September. When they arrived, things began to happen immediately. Churches opened their doors, meetings were held from church to high school auditorium to Scottish Rite Cathedral each night. People were contacted on the streets, and things began to stir. After a few weeks, the church auditoriums were filled to capacity and local pastors were crying for more help to follow up on the newly converted. I found out later that people had been praying for years for this to happen in Duluth.

Still safe and snug in Indianapolis, we got a call at the beginning of February (now 1972). "We need more music and more personnel. Can you guys come up and help?"

We were not crazy about the idea. Duluth is one of the coldest places in America in winter. Temperatures were dipping to −30 degrees with wind chills at −70. People weren't even driving to the meetings at night since no one's car would start. We wondered if our van would make it to Duluth, but we were young and without much fear and decided to go check it out. I remember that, on the drive up, once we hit the Minnesota border no matter how hard we cranked the heat we could still see our breath inside the van – and it was a brand new van. And I kept thinking, "What are we getting ourselves into?"

We played every night to a packed house. The whole Jesus People team split into 2 groups at night, with two simultaneous meetings going on at once in two different churches; e band in one church and The Sheep in another. The preacher gave the message, people came forward to give their lives to Christ and God began to speak to me: "I want you out of this band and into this ministry. I'll explain later." I loved music, and I loved playing in "e." Our future was bright, recording contracts were being offered and tours being scheduled. We were due to open for Johnny Cash in Dallas. Leave now? How could this be happening?

I refused the offer and told God He must have made some mistake. These Milwaukee Jesus People were not the people I wanted to be with and, besides, I had a blossoming new career as a Christian recording artist ahead of me. Surely He needed my services more in that arena.

I fought God for a month but was in Milwaukee by March – no guitar, no recording contract, no band, no money and no clue. My last concert with "e" was in Chicago. Following the concert, we returned to Ron's house, I packed a backpack, Ron took me out to I-94 heading north and I hitched a ride to Milwaukee. The guy who picked me up was completely stoned and offered me some. I declined; told him what I was doing, he nodded, "Cool."

Somehow I found the Jesus People commune from where I was left off in downtown Milwaukee. I remember walking a long way. I entered the office area and sat down, much to their surprise. "Are you Joe Grier" from e band?"

"Yep, I need to speak with one of the leaders. I think I'm supposed to join up with you guys."

There was no screening interview or application to fill out. I was just told to go down the hall to the big dorm where all of the "brothers" slept and grab a bunk. I remember feeling like I was dying inside;

something was breaking like an over-stressed beam in a bridge slowly giving way.

The first night in that bunk, in a room with 20 other guys, some on bunk beds, some on cots – snoring, snorting, talking in their sleep, yelling in their sleep – a world away from my comfy little den in Indianapolis. Some of them were fresh off the streets – wild-looking, unshaven – speaking Christ's name yet barely knowing their own.

One dorm buddy had a speech impediment that wouldn't allow him to say his L's so it came out "ha-way-woo-yah" and he always spoke at the top of his lungs, and he had a quick, violent temper and he looked like a super-sized, tripped-out Rowan Atkinson. Another of our denizens was 6'6" and looked like Lurch and he snored the loudest. I did not hit him in the shoulder to get him to turn over. Robbie was also 6'6" and fresh off the streets where he'd spent his recent adult years as a transvestite selling himself to whosoever. My dorm room. I had visions of dying in my bed, being strangled before even figuring out why I was there. One Flew Over the Cuckoo's Nest came out three years later but I'm pretty sure the plot and characters were hatched in that room. I might have cried that first night.

Your primary reason for existing in this commune was to occupy a street corner with a hand full of underground Jesus papers and invitations to our coffee house on Brady Street. We walked daily to downtown Milwaukee, rain and shine, cold or warm, and picked a spot and stood there waiting for God to bring the right person along. Until that happened, the conversation was pretty much one-way and directed in general to anyone in general who happened to pass by: "Hi, how are you? Jesus loves you today. Would you like a paper?"

From time to time, a person would stop to take a paper or engage in conversation. We had many interesting chats with all kinds of people and even prayed with some. We were supposed to return any donations for our papers to the home office, but since we ended up standing out there through lunch hour, I often purchased peanuts and drinks to calm my hunger. My first two months on the streets happened to be February and March 1972. The cold was brutal. I returned home to the commune one night with frostbite on a couple toes.

We lived "by faith." In other words, we lived from what was donated to us in pity by strangers on the streets and from churches in Milwaukee. I'm not saying that to be cynical, but our naïveté knew no bounds, so by faith it was. Meals consisted of watered down lentil soup, peanut butter and jelly, oatmeal and whatever else could be scrounged. It was a bit of a step down in the world for me. At least in Indianapolis we had graduated from cauliflower and butterscotch to peaches and salads.

Spreading Out

On the whole, Milwaukee wasn't much fun. We lived in the ghetto on Fourth Street just north of the old Schlitz brewery and within smelling distance of the incomparable Ambrosia chocolate factory. Each day, as I walked downtown to witness (a term meaning "to speak with passers-by about Christ; people who, for the most part, wished you'd just drop dead) on the streets with a half-full belly of lentils, I smelled an incredible mixture of smooth, brewery malt and luscious chocolate. It simply wasn't fair.

The walk downtown in the middle of winter was a cold one. Standing on the street corners for hours was chilling. The walk back up the hill toward our accommodations was painful. As I said, I got my first case of frostbite that year. The only reason any of us survived the Milwaukee deep freeze was because, with the purchase of peanut M&Ms, we were allowed to stand inside the door of the Walgreen's on Wisconsin Ave. and warm up for awhile.

There were gunshots some nights across the street – ambulances were regular visitors to the neighborhood. Our preaching was mainly to poor people who'd already heard it before or to drug burnout cases who seemed, for the most part, beyond salvage.

One day in early March, my ministry partner, Ken, (we always used the "buddy system") and I went down one street just a block off Fourth St. knocking on doors and inviting people to our coffee house for that night's festivities.

It was about 10 degrees with a chilling east wind so when we were cordially invited into a house by a slightly-built black man in his thirties, we accepted. "Come on in and tell us what you need to tell us. We'll listen."

The living room contained several well-dressed African-American women and a couple of other men. We were the only white guys within five miles. Ken looked at me, and I could tell his eyes were a little bigger than I had remembered before. I simply took it all in and, within 15 seconds, my street smart, super-powered, finely honed instincts had assessed the situation: the women weren't women. They were men dressed like women. And they were all very attentive. There was a moment when I almost grabbed Ken and ran for it. I wondered if we were going to walk out of the house, or if we would be carried out of the house.

Ken began, "I, uh, we, uh … just came by to share that Jesus loves you. He died for your sins and wants to forgive you."

They smiled and nodded their heads.

I chimed in, "We have this literature here for you if you'd like to read it."

One of the men stepped forward and thanked me.

I continued, "Tonight is our coffee house, and we'd like to invite you to come."

They nodded.

"Have any of you ever thought about giving your hearts to Jesus?"

"Oh, yes," they said. "We've thought about it." A few of them covered their mouths and laughed lightly. There was a long pause.

"Well, we hope you'll continue to think about it... and we think it's probably time to go."

Someone said, "Thanks for stopping by."

Half way down the block, I turned to Ken and said, "I think we need to pray." My knees were still weak, and my heart was still pounding. We bowed our heads, asked for calm and prayed that somehow God would use whatever it was we had just left back there in a cathouse full of transvestites.

Chapter Seven
Tent City

The two hundred plus Jesus people who squeezed into the old retirement home just north of the Schlitz brewery in Milwaukee were not destined to stay together. Three very different, very gifted, very territorial, alpha males became our leaders and eventually their personalities and callings made it impossible to continue together. So each took a part of the group and headed out from Milwaukee. Jim Palosaari took his group to Europe, John Herrin went to Florida (this group later became Jesus People, USA and settled in Chicago) and Bill Lowery went to Davenport, Iowa with his tattered gospel tent, twenty-year-old semi-truck and trailer and about sixty of us. We became over-night tent evangelists. We became over-night gypsies as well; probably leaning more gypsy than evangelist. He had painted Christ is the Answer in huge blue letters on the side of the trailer and that became our ministry's name.

Bill, our leader and former tent evangelist, discovered early that I'd been a professional musician before coming to Milwaukee, and so I was designated the worship leader. He was the preacher. I hadn't touched my guitar in weeks, so this was welcome news. There were other musicians with us, and we formed a musical team and did our best at putting together a long-haired (I do not mean classical) version of the Old Time Gospel Hour. I had to quickly familiarize myself with standards like "The Old Rugged Cross," "Down the Sawdust Trail," and "Thank You, Lord, for Saving My Soul." We went to the streets of Davenport during the day just as we had done in Milwaukee. We sang and preached and prayed at night as people streamed into the tent to hear us. The guys slept in the gospel tent at night on small, wooden, foldout chairs in sleeping bags. The girls slept in a smaller tent on foldout cots in sleeping bags. The married couples either had their own campers or small camping tents.

It was only April in Iowa, so we needed heat in the big tents. We managed to find large smudge pots - you know, the kind used in orchards to keep frost off the fruit. The pots burned kerosene and let off black smoke when they weren't working right which was most of the time. Every morning when I awoke, my eyes stung and my nostrils were full of something black, the half-combusted kerosene having left its carbon footprint up my nose.

Each day unfolded the same: up in the morning, a team meeting in the big top around 9am, while eating your oatmeal, and on the streets by 10am. I can't remember what we did for lunch at that time but I think the kitchen staff prepared peanut butter and jelly sandwiches for us to take with (when we were able to afford it).

Showers or bathing of any sort were tricky. We usually had a particular day or two in the week when it was our turn. We would load into the ministry's only van or a couple cars and head down to the YMCA, pay for our showers and head back to the tent. On weeks when there was no money, we either didn't bathe or we went to the nearest truck stop, pretended to be truckers and hoped we didn't get caught. Sometimes very kind, naïve individuals would invite a group of us to their home for showers which often ended in their not inviting us back again because of the stopped up drains and toilets. Those into self-flagellation invited us back a second and third time. It was sad, really.

As it was in Milwaukee, so it was in Davenport. There wasn't much to eat. Someone did donate a pick-up truck full of bananas: "Finish those and there's more where that came from." We'd rented a vacant parking lot on the north side of the Mississippi River on the levee and advertised, you guessed it, "Drive your Chevy to the Levee! Come hear about Jesus!"

We tent dwellers evangelized on the streets in all four of the Quad Cities: Davenport and Bettendorf, Iowa and Moline and Rock Island, Illinois. The girls met Julie on the street one night outside a hotel in downtown Moline. Julie stood six foot four inches and was gorgeous. She was a receptionist at the hotel and she used to be a man but had undergone a sex change operation - in 1972. We were absolutely not ready for Julie, but she was amazed that the girls would even talk with her; and their conversation on the street corner lasted well into the night.

They returned at suppertime to the coffee house where we were staying and the girls invited Julie to stay for supper. She did, they continued to talk and later that night Julie prayed to receive Christ into her heart. The guys were sleeping on one side of a wall made by hanging blankets over a rope, and I remember waking at one point to hear the girls congratulating Julie on becoming a believer.

Julie quit her job at the hotel the next day and moved in ... with the girls. We had urgent discussions about what to do ... I mean what are you going to do? Bunk this beautiful woman in with the guys? Nuh uh.

She stayed awhile but could not travel with us. We learned later that Julie had become a librarian in Des Moines, Iowa, still a Christian and still celibate. Wow.

We moved from Davenport, IA to Decatur, IL and had the same rousing success in Decatur. Seriously! Large numbers of people came to the meetings; many young people received Christ; many were prayed with on the street corners. As it had been in Duluth and Davenport, so it was in Decatur. And we still slept in tents and sleeping bags and took showers whenever and wherever we could. From these beginnings, Christ is the Answer took shape. By the end of our Decatur meetings, which ran well through June and into July, we numbered over a hundred and left town with two more semi-trucks, two Greyhound buses and an assortment of other vehicles.

We also made Weldon, Illinois our worldwide headquarters during our stay in Decatur. Our leader, Bill, had grown up in Weldon and had purchased the old school building just before meeting up with us. It was actually a pretty nice building for an antique – three aboveground floors, nice toilets and showers in the basement and plenty of space on the playground to park campers, buses, trucks, cars and semi-trucks; a four-foot-diameter fire escape tube running from floor number three to the street. There was a nice little park across one side street with lots of nice shade trees and a five-and-dime across the other side street. We never really found out from the locals what they thought when we came to town.

Really, what would you think? Weldon, Illinois – population 429 on a good day with a total area of .3 square miles. Then the gypsies came to town after the meetings finished in Decatur and by the next morning, the Weldon population had ballooned to 550. Girls in long, granny-gown dresses and young men in torn blue jeans and very long hair cavorted and lounged and read their Bibles and played their guitars in the city park. You could try to do the movie about this, but you'd never be able to capture the thoughts and emotions of the Weldon locals in those days.

Gayle and I would live like this for the next eleven years: city to city, country to country – always in tents and sleeping bags, no paycheck, traveling in trucks and buses, doing ministry in a very unusual way – the "foxes have holes, birds have nests" illustration that Jesus used. He had nowhere to lay His precious head. At least we had sleeping bags.

Chapter Eight
Farther Along

During our time in Decatur and short layover in Weldon, we managed to pick up a few people/things: mainly more gypsies, which also meant more mobile housing. So we purchased two very old semi-trucks and two very old Greyhound buses, which enlarged the caravan to about fifteen separate vehicles. Some of the newcomers actually owned vehicles so they signed them over to us and watched as newly hatched, well-meaning team members who had never owned a vehicle themselves, drove what had been a well-maintained car or truck into the ground. Oil changes? Who knew? "Why does the pointer always go from C to H on that one dial? Does that mean something ... you know ... when it gets close to H?"

We headed for Aurora, Illinois. Bill knew people who knew people and somehow managed to secure an amazing tent location in a beautiful city park on Aurora's south side. What a site and what a sight! Again, the nightly meetings were wonderful; the tent full of people from the area curious to see what was going on. Our music team had expanded so I now had band mates, including the aforementioned Mark and Debbie Gungor – Mark on keyboards and Debbie singing along with my wife-to-be, Gayle. We also acquired Dave the drummer from Racine, WI (recently freed from heroine addiction) and Chuck the bass player from Duluth, MN. So it was rock 'n roll time in the old tent meeting!

It seemed like hippies drew hippies in those early days. We did not cut our hair or try to alter our appearance to please anyone; we just let everything grow. Once the word got out in the community that hippies were playing rock under a tent in the city park every night, it would attract our element and amazing things would happen.

Jared Worby had heard about us through friends and, along with a couple of his buddies, managed to make their way to the meetings one night, severely handicapped under the influence of a heaping helping of alcohol. Jared later told me that his sole purpose was to come out, check out the chicks and see if he could hook up. His mission was short-lived, however, due to a conflicting Intent with a conflicting Agenda, and something akin to a miracle transformed him before he left the park. He was with us on the streets the next day. Jared is still serving in the ministry in Romania, still testifying about that night when God the Agenda with great Intent, met him "in-tent."

We had our first public baptism in Aurora, in a local pond in a local park. There were so many people wanting to take that next step of faith that day that we had to form two lines. Bill waded out, then I waded out and then the people waded out in two lines to meet us. I baptized Jared and many others - unforgettable.

Chapter Nine
Much Farther Along

It was now deep summer, 1972, and somehow we came to the conclusion that the next city to invade would be Topeka, Kansas. We had grown to a good number and had acquired more vehicles in Aurora so it was off to Topeka via Interstate 80, Interstate 35 and Interstate 70.

If you're in any kind of ministry, sooner or later you will travel. It comes with the territory. Jesus and the twelve were always moving somewhere. Preachers' families are probably second only to military families in frequency of relocation. We traveled constantly for eleven years. Of course when you travel, you get to see a lot of new things and experience all kinds of experiences. Travel magazines describe this kind of life as exotic and exciting. It was all of that. There are other "e" words that also come to mind.

In the course of those eleven years we circled the globe twice and probably the equivalent of another couple of circles just going back and forth.

We collected vehicles from the very beginning. It was our second passion. We started with the two old Greyhound buses and a semi, then added a couple of semis and assorted other vehicles in each town as we went along. Each married couple joining us along the way brought their own camping trailer with something to tow it. And there were numerous auxiliary vehicles – pickup trucks, vans, cars and a "pooper-scooper." We made that one ourselves: an old 500 gallon fuel tank welded to the back of a two-ton pick-up; hoses in and hoses out coupled with a vacuum pump that ran off the truck engine and a release valve. It was glorious.

There was an old Pepsi semi-trailer, which our mechanics converted into six porta-potty stalls. Since we had our own pooper-scooper, we could empty our own porta-potties. The "honey dew" truck only ran sometimes, which meant the porta-potties were only emptied sometimes.

A 44 foot-long semi-trailer was converted into a kitchen and laundry room. The back two-thirds was the kitchen. It was actually pretty nice. It had commercial grade ovens and sinks, hardwood flooring and a couple nice refrigerators. The cooks did their best, but there's something incongruous about a commercial kitchen being used day after day for the manufacture of oatmeal, peanut butter and jelly and spaghetti. Those were our staples because that's all we could afford.

We drained the wastewater from the kitchen and laundry into whatever was available. I do remember that when we got to California, the health officials went wild and shut us down for a few days. We had to hold it.

Another of our semi-trailers was converted into a shower facility, one side for men and the other for women. It had been a refrigerator trailer before, so the floor was ribbed aluminum. The shower truck was fine until winter. I remember taking showers when I could see my breath and the drains had to be periodically cleared of ice. And there were times when there wasn't enough money to buy propane to run the water heater. And there was no insulation under the floor, really, so one either wore flip-flops or walked gingerly.

Later an office semi-trailer and a generator trailer were added. The generator trailer had two huge diesel generators, one for our camp and one for the array of lights in the main tent. Only one of those generators usually worked, so we often did without electricity in the camp; you know, just like you do when you go camping, the only difference being ... well, this wasn't camping; more like surviving. Like I said earlier, we called it living by faith. Einstein's definition of insanity comes to mind: "Doing the same thing over and over again and expecting different results." When you're convinced that what you're doing and the way you're doing it has great merit, it's easy to repeat certain behaviors, like camping for a cause.

All of the semi-trailers had Christ is the Answer written in huge letters across the sides, so everyone saw us coming. We traveled together in caravan and, at the height of our days on the road, had 250 people and 13 semi trucks and trailers. Imagine seeing 13 semis going down the highway emblazoned with Christ is the Answer – a moving Burma Shave ad for God.

Truck stops, obviously, became a regular hangout between cities. They didn't like us, even though we bought a lot of diesel fuel and gasoline. We looked bad to start with: long hair; torn, dirty blue jeans. And after a few days on the road, we didn't just look bad! We would virtually monopolize the showers and the rest rooms when we moved into a truck stop.

There might have been something redemptive about our truck stop visits if we'd bought food at their restaurants. Well, we did in a way, if you can imagine 250 people drinking coffee and then going out to the trucks to get their peanut butter and jelly sandwiches.

Many of our members were denied access to the truckers' showers because they were not truck drivers. That was never a problem. We would simply go into the regular bathrooms, strip down to our underwear and bathe in the sinks. Of course we didn't condone our people doing this, nevertheless we managed to get booted out of a few truck stops.

Today, when I turn on a shower and warm water comes out, and I'm able to get clean, I often give thanks. Truck stops taught us to appreciate the simpler things in life.

None of the vehicles were new. All of the vehicles had at least ten years each on them. And so there were breakdowns – lots of breakdowns. We had CB radios in the caravan, so when a vehicle broke down, we'd radio ahead to the leader, he'd stop the caravan, and the mechanics took a look.

A breakdown could take days to fix. So we got used to camping along side highways and interstates and waiting. Sometimes people became separated from the caravan for whatever reason and broke down while separated. We wouldn't hear from them for days and even weeks. Sometimes, if they had no money, people in towns would take them in out of pity. Sometimes they simply got discouraged, phoned mom and dad, got a bus ticket home and abandoned the vehicle.

In retrospect I don't really blame them.

There were numerous accidents over the years. Put an ex-hippie in a semi with little or no commercial driving experience and stuff happens. In Las Vegas, one of our semi drivers lost control of his truck as he was negotiating an interstate off ramp near downtown. His brakes failed, he pulled the trailer brakes so they'd lock and then went crashing into the guardrail. The truck stopped and dangled over the side of the ramp, suspended above the roadway underneath, and the dangling truck spit him out. He came away with a couple of broken legs, as I recall, but it could have been much worse.

Chapter Ten
The Summer of 1972

We camped in Topeka, Kansas. Topeka was the origination point of the Pentecostal revival that broke out in the early 1900s. Agnes Ozman, a student at Pastor Charles Parham's Bethel Bible College, began speaking in tongues on New Year's Eve, 1900 during a student prayer meeting. Another student of Parham's, William Seymour, would later move to Los Angeles and start his own Pentecostal church on Azusa Street where another revival began among Seymour's fellow African-American brothers and sisters. The Azusa Revival mushroomed into something far greater than what happened in Topeka, but the seeds were planted on the plains of Kansas.

It would have been a wonderful thing to experience the same sort of revival during our meetings in Topeka that had accompanied the preaching of Charles Parham, but it was not to be, and we moved south to Tulsa, Oklahoma. Tulsa was and is quite a place. The Pentecostalism that began in Topeka migrated south just as we had and found fertile ground in the midst of an Oklahoma oil boom. Oral Roberts, the famous tent evangelist and the university by the same name are located in Tulsa. Our landing in Tulsa was different than Oral's, however.

Before moving to a new city with our tent city, it became necessary to send scouts ahead to spy out the land and locate suitable places. "Suitable" for us meant at least an acre's area, access to public electricity, water and roads and, hopefully, land that was high enough above sea level that there was no danger of flooding. Tulsa offered none of those amenities. We found that out too late; camp had already been struck in Topeka and the tent city was on its way south. All that Tulsa offered was the empty grounds of a shutdown drive-in theater on the city's north side. We took it because there was nothing else.

The tent went up without a hitch but it was September going into October in Oklahoma and the summer had not yet worked thunderstorms out of its system. There was one doozy left, and it hit the day that the tent was put up. We retreated for cover into the trucks and campers as the storm hit. The abandoned drive-in lot was located on the top of a high hill overlooking Tulsa to the south and the winds hit us full force. Before the tent could be lowered, the storm shred the canvas into strips and pieces and the whole thing collapsed into the mud. The entire campsite turned into a swamp. No tent, no meetings, no money.

Word spread quickly throughout Tulsa that a tent city inhabited by Jesus People on the north side had become a mud city: people without food or shelter, babies without diapers, moms with nowhere to wash clothes. And what respectable news station would pass up a chance to catch this mush of misery on camera? And so they came, and the news hit TV stations that night and we were overnight celebrities. By the next day individuals were driving to the top of the hill to bring supplies, but even more dramatic, the Red Cross came to the camp with soup and blankets and declared us a disaster area.

I don't remember much about the aftermath of the thunderstorm. We did manage to find another tent, we had meetings, we survived on Red Cross soup and the meetings were quite successful. We were also thrown in jail. That's easy to remember.

Shopping malls had gained in popularity across the country and there was a large one in Tulsa. We began to see a shift in where people went to do their shopping and their socializing – away from downtown and out to the malls, which made sense. The malls were closer to the suburbs; all of the stores were right there in one spot; the parking lots were enormous and free – what was not to like? This also made it more difficult to find people to speak with on the downtown street corners with the American mall explosion in full bloom, and the downtown street corner formerly known as "gospel opportunity" drying up. Unless you wanted to speak with drunks, homeless drunks or busy lawyers, evangelism just wasn't happening in Tulsa.

But the malls, now that was different - a temperature-controlled environment, tons of people patronizing the new American marketplace, benches where people could sit, rest and talk about God – what was not to like? The immediate problem we discovered was that malls, unlike downtown street corners, were not totally public places. Most malls were zoned as quasi-public, which meant that they were a little bit of private and a little bit of public. At the new American mall you were welcome to shop and eat, but sitting on a bench and reading to someone from a Bible, not so much; not at all, as a matter of fact.

But this was where the people were, and this was where we were determined to go, and so we did. On our first day at the mall, it lasted, I think, a total of three hours max, at which point the mall security people approached to inform us that "soliciting" in the mall was not permitted and against the law – "trespassing" was the official term they used, and what pure-hearted disciple of Jesus would want to be arrested for public trespassing, and so we left ... on the first day.

That night, however, the more militant among us began to question the legitimacy of the mall patrol's claims. "Maybe it was a fluke," we thought. "Maybe those guys were just having a bad day and took it out on us. Let's try again."

But on the next day, the security patrol was still in a foul mood and warned us again; only this time we decided to test their sincerity and earnestness and kept moving around the mall, staying in only one place for a few minutes and then moving on; cat and mouse – it was actually pretty funny. But it didn't work. They caught our scent, they searched us out and said that we had ten minutes to leave the mall property or the Tulsa police would be called in. Layin' down that gauntlet.

This just got us riled; we rose to the challenge and stayed our ground and were whisked off to jail. The challenges and responses escalated in the coming days to where close to half our entourage was in jail (and eating quite well I might add). Lawyers came forward offering help, trial dates were set (quickly since we were not posting bail and the jail was becoming more crowded by the day) and our group of jailbirds were convicted of trespassing, fined and let go for time served. The Tulsa news media absolutely loved us.

This mall situation began to play itself out in every city – we'd show up at a mall to speak with people about their faith, hand out fliers inviting them to our nightly meetings and end up in jail. But we got wiser in the process and learned that the whole anti-solicitation charge and trespassing charge (which were inevitably brought against us) were unconstitutional; that a mall area, being "quasi-public" was also a free-speech zone where any U.S. citizen was free to speak their mind as long as there was no security problem.

Of course "quasi-public free speech zone" was a brand new concept in free speech, so in each new city we encountered security personnel who were unwilling to accept our constitutional discovery and arrested us anyway. All trespass cases subsequently brought against us in every city were eventually dismissed; we were freed from jail (we never posted bail) and back to the malls we would go. We learned later from one security officer, that, had we sued the mall where we'd been arrested, and where he worked, we could have owned it.

With Tulsa in the rearview mirror and a few new group members and a few more vehicles, we went south to Austin, Texas. We were able to locate a small vacant lot between two storefronts very close to the University of Texas campus. There is something about a campus town that makes faith difficult. We saw it often no matter where we traveled: university campus + university people x arrogance to a factor of 4 = 0. At least that was our experience. Campus ministries were much more successful than we were. They had devised strategies for flying under the secular, hate-a-Christian radar, which was the opposite of how we functioned. We didn't know what flying under the radar meant. And so, the method of walking right up to a person and discussing issues of faith with them on a city sidewalk in Milwaukee bombed when attempted in Austin. We were scorned, scolded and ignored.

But NOT, for some reason, once the meetings in the tent began – word got out on the Austin street – the circus was in town and was recruiting performers. So each night during the meetings different uninvited hopefuls came for their presumptive auditions – Cirque du Soleil washouts.

We set up a ramp with a landing right in front of the main stage running parallel alongside the stage. You could go up one side of the ramp, hit the landing and then proceed down the exit side of the ramp. We used it at the end of the service for people who wanted to come forward for prayer ... or auditions.

Night number one, audition number one - someone rode a full size horse into the tent, up the ramp and back down during the service.

Night number two, audition two – a different person rode a motorcycle up the ramp and on out the opposite side of the tent, during the service.

Night number three, audition three – someone strewed into the tent during worship, up to the stage, stood on his head and began accompanying the worship team on the flute.

I don't really remember much from Austin besides the bizarre events during the meetings. The hardness and resistance we encountered from people on campus was an exercise in frustration and, at times, humiliation: rejection times a thousand.

Jesus told his disciples there would be both receptive and unreceptive cities and towns. He experienced the cold shoulder more than once; sometimes a cold shoulder bordering on violence. Nazareth, Capernaum, Bethsaida, Gadara,

Jerusalem – resistance and rejection were not new to him hence the warning to his followers.

Rejection is the hardest thing about evangelism and evangelism is what we did. Our whole reason for existing was to tell others; we came to your town to broadcast the good news that Jesus loves you and why would you not want to hear that? There were a few in our group who could handle the rejection, particularly the ones who were our most gifted orators; who could sell anything, chat up anyone and make the whole world love the bitter medicine as they spooned it in. But most of us, including me, were not so gifted, and to encounter rejection was really, really painful. What do you do if you want the world to like you; if you just want to get along; if you'd rather have friends than enemies; if you just want things to go peacefully? And then you're called upon to approach someone with a message that arouses nothing but disdain and repulsion. No thank you.

We called it "going to the streets," and it was the most distasteful activity of my whole time in that ministry, from the streets of Milwaukee to Austin and points beyond. Going to the streets? More like going to hell for me. Some of us saw the "streets" as a challenge so they attacked it as you would a threatening adversary. Others woke up every day believing that they were going to meet people who would absolutely love them and welcome their conversation; a warm tête-à-tête with an old friend. I never could get my head around their optimism.

I remember reading stories of Christian ministers who would sit down next to someone on a plane, start a conversation about God and end up leading that person in a prayer as they sat there sobbing for joy. I tried the same thing on planes, and the person would turn silent or move across the aisle. It made me feel bad. I was an introvert by nature (like most musicians) and my insides screamed objection when I thought of approaching someone I'd never met with a gospel for which they had no felt need. It was awful. I did it anyway but never enjoyed it. I always looked for excuses to get out of doing street time and had no problem handling the guilt associated with feeling that way. Once out there, I was rejected 95% of the time so Jesus' warning about rejection was something I learned well. We survived; it was okay; but it was so distasteful. Just being honest.

It was a relief for us to continue moving south, which we did as the southern winter was getting ready to kick in, and Austin hissed "good riddance" as we left town. San Antonio, Texas – San Pedro Avenue – a major north-south city byway at that time and a great place for a tent meeting.

Everything we had experienced in Austin found its opposite in San Antonio. We were a weird sight in every city we entered, but San Antonio seemed okay with weird. From our first day until the last, we knew that we'd been embraced and appreciated. The most astonishing thing was the response from people we met on the streets. They wanted to stop and talk and listen, and hundreds, maybe thousands, not only listened but bowed their heads and hearts in prayer with us. We started counting, and realized we were averaging 90-100 people per day praying to ask Jesus into their hearts.

We were invited to participate in weekend outreach to denizens of downtown San Antonio at a coffee house called the Green Gate. We learned that it had previously been a strip joint but that the owners (a man and wife) and customers had been waylaid one night by a street preacher who ventured into the club, spoke to everyone gathered around the bar and prayed with the man and wife to receive Christ. It became a coffee house.

Leo Ramos joined our happy warrior band a few days before we left San Antonio along with a few other stragglers. Leo had been a platoon sergeant in Viet Nam and had watched as his whole platoon was massacred in an ambush. He'd been drunk for several years since; just couldn't get over the nightmare and the survivor's guilt. He sauntered into the meetings, had a God encounter and joined up.

Weighing in at 220 pounds on a 5'7" frame, Leo was a walking enigma. Beneath the Poncho Villa mustache and the well-groomed, well-oiled hair lay a sadness and anger that none of us ever figured out. "Joe," he would say. "Paisano. Look at my face. There is nothing but love written on this face for you. Do you believe me?" Of course paisano is from a Spanish idiom which means compatriot, but in the Southwest it also doubles as Mexican slang for the roadrunner, and I never figured out which one he meant.

"Paisano. Look at my face. There is nothing but love written on this face for you. Do you believe me?"

To which I would reply, "Yes, Leo, I believe you," with a twitch of discomfort streaking across my sixth sense because I'd seen this kind of verbal exchange in The Godfather and because when someone has your trust why would they need to ask? And this response was, without fail, then accompanied by Leo dragging me toward him in a manly, Corleone-type abrazo.

Leo knew that he did not have my trust. Oh, and one thing he had forgotten to tell us was that he was running from the Mob, that he'd been a Mob hit man and saw us as the perfect cover. Leo, my paisano, a for real road runner. More about that later.

Chapter 11
Urban Deserts

*I like the desert for short periods of time,
from inside a car, with the windows rolled
up, and the doors locked. I prefer
beach resorts with room service.*
- Anne Lamott

Leo and the caravan closed up shop in "San Antone"
and headed west to Phoenix, Arizona, 982 miles of
straight four-lane ribbon through the desert
southwest.

We encountered stiff west winds and an upward
climb toward the peak of the Continental Divide.
There were breakdowns and separations and
difficult times as always, but the desert was a
foreign place for most of us, so add disorientation
into the mix. Endless Midwest cornfields were one
thing; endless sand was intimidating.

All through our time in the Southwest it was
something new – heat, hot wind, sand, cacti, lizards,
centipedes, scorpions, rattle snakes and the most
beautiful sunsets I'd ever seen. Gayle and I would
end up living in the desert for seven years, and
despite the hardship and the heat, you begin to
appreciate the beauty.

Come upon a stream winding its way through a northern forest under the shadow of a green canopy and listen to the forest's many voices and smell the evergreen – it's easy to see and hear God there. But God is not who comes to mind when you wake up in the cab of a semi and look out on – well, desert nothing. You see a mile or two of sand and hills in every direction and your built-in GPS-amometer tells you without hesitation: "After those first two miles there are three hundred more just like it; no gas stations, no wells, no water. Have a nice day." That's all you hear. The inner voice gives way to emotional discomfort which gives way to restlessness which gives way to lightning bursts of fear: "How long will I be broken down in this mess? Who knows I'm here? Bathrooms? Water?"

Living outside in tents in the desert, sometimes on the ground or close to the ground, Bedouin-like, was really challenging and UNcomfortable. We set up in downtown Phoenix but that didn't matter. It was still an urban desert and dust and sand were everywhere. Nothing stops the wind in the desert therefore nothing stops the sand; not skyscrapers, not office buildings. It blew into the tent all night long depositing a fine layer on everything: sleeping bags, pillows, chairs, hair, skin, shoes, vehicles; and woe to the person who sleeps with the mouth open. The fallout was endless. We quickly adapted to checking inside shoes and sleeping bags and blue jeans ever day because urban scorpions and urban black widows loved those dark, smelly places.

Phoenix was the most unusual city. We learned that, in the winter, Phoenix was like a crossroads for people going to and coming from California and Texas. It was a gathering place for drifters, drunks, homeless and other disenfranchised people who found the summer-like climate very agreeable in December and January. And these were the ones we often met on the streets and who often wandered into our tent at night, near downtown on Central Avenue.

Pierre drifted in with the desert sand one day. Pierre was also a hit man for the mafia – five foot eight, wiry and compact, bald on top, sunglasses; Bruce Willis' twin brother. He joined us, too. So now we had San Antonio Leo, the hit man and Phoenix Pierre, the hit man. Our posts in the Want Ads were working: two for two. First San Antonio – hit man. Now Phoenix – hit man. Jackpot. Daily Double! We gave Pierre and Leo their own human resources tent with special consultation hours for anyone wanting to hook up with our traveling ministry. "So, you want to join up, eh? Go check with Leo and Pierre."

Shortly after Pierre showed up, so did Napoleon. Now Napoleon wasn't his real name, but he thought it was. He was extremely violent, undoubtedly schizophrenic and thought nothing of coming into the tent at night to harass our ushers or night guards. More than once he stood up to interrupt the preaching.

One night stands out. He came to worship dressed in old military garb, gold epaulets, tricorne and black boots. And, as was his custom, Napoleon stood during worship and began proclaiming his sovereignty over the masses. He also brought an extra prop – a for-freaking-real, gleaming, steel sword with an edge. He proceeded to pull it from its scabbard, turned to those around him and began swinging violently: "Off with their heads!"

I was leading worship. I just kept singing and Napoleon kept on swinging. I was becoming jaded, unflappable. Our ushers made it to him before he could hurt anyone, which was a small miracle in itself. One of our larger men, B.J., wrestled him to the ground, got the sword away and ended up paying for his heroism with bruises and scrapes. Napoleon had to be held on the ground until the police came. You just never knew what you might get under that tent – a circus without the clowns, acrobats, elephants and makeup.

Pierre remained with us only during the time in Phoenix but decided to stay back. A few weeks later, on a return trip to Phoenix, one of our team members ran into Pierre on a street corner. They had friendly conversation. We had hoped Pierre would go on with us to California, but he kept insisting he had unfinished business in Phoenix and that maybe we'd see him later. "Oh, and by they way," he said in passing as our team member began walking away. " Remember 'Napoleon?' I happened to see him in an alley the other night, and we took a walk. You won't have to worry about him any more." That Pierre.

Hit man number three paid us a visit during our stay in Phoenix; on reflection they must have had their own union hall. We'd set up shop in front of a couple pornography businesses on the south side, marching slowly back and forth with a smile to passersby and an invitation to our meetings at night directed especially to men exiting the shop. The owner of one store was beside himself. His business had been severely affected and prospective clients, upon seeing the freaks with Bibles, drove right on by. (By the way, you wouldn't believe the number of church deacons and youth pastors we've met coming out of those shops over the years. Ugh.) The owner called the police to have us arrested for trespassing (which drew a real snicker from the cops), then, after a few days, came out breathing threats, cursing and chasing after some of us with a bat. Nothing worked for the poor guy; we just kept coming back like roaches in a desert shack; it was a public sidewalk and we were simply exercising our freedom of speech.

What we didn't know was that this owner had connections to underworld figures in Phoenix; Pierre-type figures. He wasted no time hiring one such person and sent him to the tent one night with a loaded .45 with orders to take out the preacher while he stood on the stage. We had no idea who the man was.

The strangest thing happened. The singing and worship time went without a hitch; then the sermon and then the nightly altar call (an invitation to those attending to come forward for prayer if they'd been touched by the message). What we did not know was that, among the crowd coming forward, was the very tall, very dangerous hit man; and he was weeping, breaking down like a baby. A couple of the guys placed their hands on his shoulders, he bowed, they prayed and this came out of his mouth:

"I can't do it. I just can't do it!"
To which our praying brothers responded, "Yes you can. Yes you can!"

All three went to their knees. He turned to B.J. (yep, B.J. again, poor guy) and said, "You don't understand. This is what I mean." And he pulled the hidden .45 out of his belt and held it up. "I was supposed to kill that guy tonight (pointing to Bill as he prayed for the penitent). I can't do it. I'm supposed to get $4,000 for this."

"Would you give it to me before we pray?" B.J. asked. B.J. motioned to me to come over, gave me the weapon and asked me to do something with it as they prayed with the broken would-be assassin. I carried it in a supplicant's pose on both of my hands to the back of the tent and placed it carefully in the dust. We were all so stunned we forgot about the gun. We never saw the guy or the gun again.

Like I said, the hit man Want-Ad worked great.

Chapter 12
San Berdoo

Our next port of destiny was San Bernardino, California. San Berdoo (southern California speak) is a far-eastside suburb attached to the massive Los Angeles sprawl. It is the last semi-green place you see as you continue east along Interstate 10 toward Palm Springs; but what an awesome sight for us as we pulled out of the desert coming the other way and into the warm December air and smog of southern California.

We'd managed to finagle a small open lot on a major east-west thoroughfare in town and received a conditional permit from the city to set things up. What most cities chose to overlook, namely a health permit, San Bernardino chose to put under a microscope. In retrospect it really is amazing that we were permitted to function in any city, let alone San B. By this time we had multiple campers and many more people. There were children and babies multiplying weekly, a shower truck which normally drained onto the ground, a kitchen truck whose waste water also drained onto the ground and a pooper scooper for our porta-potties which worked only some of the time. Figure in the campers whose waste water drained onto the ground and whose sewage holding tanks were very small, you can see how third world we'd become.

By that time it was January 1973, we'd been together and on the road for almost nine months and were growing accustomed to our gypsy life. Any respect we'd had toward normal human sanitation had gone out the window somewhere near the Continental Divide. The San Bernardino health inspectors took one look at our setup and red-tagged everything.

"You can't be here," they said. "Move out now."

"Where can we go? The city already gave us a permit to occupy this lot," we replied.

"I don't know and I don't care. You just need to go."

Negotiations ensued, we managed to get them to agree to give us some time to get things adjusted so we could hook up to city water and a city sewer line; we changed some drains and faucets and proceeded toward the start date for meetings.

The fire department, seeing smoke from the health department and knowing there must be a fire, came out to inspect the tent and the fire extinguishers in the tent and in the kitchen truck, etc. Everyone wanted to be a star. It was Los Angeles.

Once we got going it was a good time ... until Anton LaVey heard that we'd pulled into town. What a guy, that Anton. He was high priest of the Satanic Church and author of the Satanic Bible. His headquarters was in San Bernardino. We discovered during opening week that Anton and his church of Satan had been fasting and praying for us since we'd first come to town. Now that's commitment. His disciples would begin showing up around 7:15 each night, surround the tent as the meetings were starting and then begin chanting and casting spells against us. The gall.

We invited them to come into the meetings and try out their incantations inside. They tried to enter the tent, but could get no further than the side flaps before something forced them back. That was the first night. They kept showing up but absolutely refused any offer to come closer after that night. Hmmm.

I believe they did their damage, though. "How?" you ask. Intimacy with the supernatural stretches some peoples' credulity beyond what it can bear, a switch goes off, and they can no longer accept. Skepticism sets in and, in many cases, with good reason. Much of this book leans on an assumption that there is another way to look at things; that supernatural, meaning "beyond natural," is pretty much the norm in Kingdom life and we experienced supernatural on a regular basis.

A large group of our kids left the ministry during that time and went with a whacked-out group (said the pot to the tea kettle) called The Local Church. We learned later on that many of those had left the Christian faith entirely and given up on God – a sobering reminder to us then and now that the devil goes about as a roaring lion seeking whom he may devour and, yes, he does have teeth and he did hear Anton's prayers.

Next destination – Las Vegas, Nevada – Sin City USA – Lost Vegas!

Chapter 13
What Happens in Vegas ...

Las Vegas marks itself out by nothingness. All the negative descriptions that can generally be used in labeling a city apply to it, for its absence of consistency actually makes its existence doubtful: no man's land, waste ground, non-place, ghost town, urban simulacrum, nowhere city, etc. For us it is Zeropolis, the non-city which is the very first city, just as zero is the very first number. The nothing that counts, the nothingness of neon." - Bruce Begout, Zeropolis.

The reason you should go to Las Vegas is because, for only the second time, the second time, ever, they have rebuilt Sodom and Gomorrah. It's back!! And you have the opportunity to see it before it turns to salt. - Lewis Black, The White Album

What a crazy place to engage in the kind of ministry we practiced. What was different about Vegas was that we had no place to go. We just kind of showed up on the outskirts of town, found a vacant spot in the desert and pulled the trucks and campers in. We spent the next three weeks trying to find a location in town where we could set up the entourage; but sit and wait? No sir, we did not sit and wait. We plunged head first into Sodom.

Only it wasn't exactly Sodom; Vegas was more like a large carnival for adults that had set down roots; the non-city that Bruce Begout talks about. By the time we arrived there were two midways – downtown and "The Strip." For me the lights and dazzle were impressive, but without a musical sound track it was nothing more than lots of people, lots of traffic and what seemed like a headlong rush on to the next buzz.

We began taking our positions on downtown street corners and along The Strip. We passed out Christian literature and shared with passersby that God loved them – even in this dark place. Within the first week we'd run into quite a cross section: boozers, losers, winners, addicts (the gambling kind), prostitutes, Midwesterners on vacation, dancers, street people, homeless, dealers, church deacons and … police.

It didn't take long, maybe three days, before security noticed our presence on the sidewalks in front of the casinos, figured out what we were doing and called the cops. At first we were given the usual stern talk: "You can't be here; you're trespassing; you can't harass customers, etc." Of course this was different than being in a shopping mall. We were on city streets, public sidewalks, not blocking anyone's passage. We, the legal eagles, knew by this time that we were well within our citizen's rights but, nevertheless, found ourselves well within the confines of the city's jail.

What was difficult for the police – there were so many of us (over 150 adults by this time), that four or five being arrested on one day only meant that those four or five would be replaced the next day. And so we kept coming and they kept arresting. By the time there were seventy of us in the clink, even Las Vegas took notice. Our faces and stories were in the paper almost every day – front page. The mayor and chief of police were calling us in trying to find a compromise so that the incarcerations wouldn't have to go on: Las Vegas – trying to save face by negotiating with people who had no face to save.

It grew comical – in one news article the police chief was quoted: " We know that they have over a thousand camped on the outskirts of the town and as many as 5,000 more on the way but we will not let these people take over our city!"

We remembered what was written in Leviticus:

You will pursue your enemies, and they will fall by the sword before you. Five of you will chase a hundred, and a hundred of you will chase ten thousand, and your enemies will fall by the sword before you.

I will look on you with favor and make you fruitful and increase your numbers, and I will keep my covenant with you. - Leviticus 26:7-9

I spent a week in jail, some of us spent longer. Because we were so many, they had to mix us in with other inmates. Willie Lewis, an amazing black man, had come to Christ during an outreach we conducted at the very beginning in Gary, Indiana. Willie was on drugs and leading an awful life; but, after his salvation experience, was a completely new person, and he followed us to our Milwaukee headquarters. Willie was our boldest evangelist; an irresistible force in the best sense of that phrase, no fear and a guileless connector.

In jail Willie was an absolute delight. He sang almost non-stop, praising God with his beautiful, smoky tenor; praying out loud for the other inmates and preaching from his jail cell to his unseen congregation in the other cells. Day and night – Pastor Willie ministering to his captive church whether they liked it or not. Like he often said of being jailed: "Great place to preach. Where they gonna go?"

One man in particular hated us in that jail. He was a junky coming down off of a terrible heroin withdrawal and a dealer who had made his living selling this poison. He was in the last cell on the block and it was very good that the jailers chose not to put any of us in there with him. He shouted and cursed and threatened: "Wait'll I see you; wait'll I get outta here; shut up, freak, 'foe I whoop yo ass!" But Willie just kept on and after a few days wore the dude down. He ended up praying with the guy (they were in adjoining cells) to receive Jesus ... at least I think that's what happened ... or the guy prayed in order to shut Willie up. Fat chance.

As in every city, we were growing wiser concerning

our free speech rights and we were soon released from jail. They pleaded with us not to go back to the casino sidewalks; and in some cases where we had encountered too much traffic and not much response, we complied.

Leo was still with us, still using us as a cover on his flight from the Mob. This was awkward, right? Typically, a man in his shoes leaves Las Vegas; he does not come to Las Vegas and stand on street corners speaking about Jesus ... with television cameras rolling.

We learned that one afternoon, a long, black limousine pulled up to the curb where Leo was standing, the door opened, a pause; then Leo got in. Some of the team members, returning from the streets that afternoon, told me what had happened and I started wondering what in the world was going on. And then Leo called – "can you come pick me up downtown" which I did, and on our way back he spilled the beans. He'd been using us as a cover the whole time; he'd been seen by some old mafia friends; they'd picked him up and taken him to a basement parking garage under one of the casinos just to catch up on old times and then let him go. He was shaken; as sober as I'd ever seen him but had managed to convince his associates that the new gig with us was for real.

We got a phone call from a "business man" a few days later asking me if I'd meet him in front of the Four Aces downtown; that he was involved with the casino and was hoping we could talk about why we were continuing to occupy space on "their" sidewalk. I didn't get his name. As I was walking out of the house we were using for a temporary office, Leo asked, "Where you going, compadre?"

"Downtown. A guy called and wants to meet me in front of the Four Aces to talk about working out a deal between us and the casino."

"You are not going to that meeting, Joe."

"Why not? He just wants to talk."

"You are not going, and I'll put you down on the floor if I have to, but you can't go there."

Leo knew things that I did not know about Mob intimidation. He'd learned that we had crossed the line with the unknown "casino powers" and that there would be no more negotiations; just a sawed off shotgun stuck out of the window of a passing car; Blam! Brother Joe goes down; problem solved.

We found a decent tent location and began meetings almost four weeks after we'd arrived in town. It was interesting to meet those attending who'd seen us in the paper or on TV. They were from all walks of life: show girls, plumbers, teachers, mechanics, and housewives. All kinds. We began to see that Las Vegas, for all the hoopla, was really a city like every other city – inhabited by real humans with real needs and many searching for a better way of life.

The city itself was very two-dimensional and flaky. The people were the opposite once we got to know them and pray with them. In spite of the nightmare of life in the desert – the wind, the heat and the dust – and the mirage that passed as happiness in the casinos, the people who made Las Vegas home were very much three-dimensional, very much human, and God was there on a wager with the dark side that many of these people could find redemption.

Chapter 14
Nashville and Its Cats

The summer of '73 was filled with a long drive from Vegas to Denver, meetings in Denver and then another long drive back to headquarters in Weldon, Illinois before hitting the road again for Nashville, Tennessee.

Music City USA, founded in 1779 on the banks of the Cumberland River, was named after Brigadier General Francis Nash, a Revolutionary War hero killed in 1777 at the battle of Germantown, PA. It was the first southern capital city to fall to Union armies during the Civil War and later became home to an amazing array of post-secondary education learning institutions; twenty-four currently.

It was the heart of country music for decades and the Ryman Auditorium, home of the original Grand Ole Opry, still stands and hosts frequent concerts along with the Grande Ole Opry in winter months.

Because of its many college-level schools it is also known as the Parthenon of the South after the seat of learning in ancient Greece located on Mars Hill in Athens. It's also been labeled the "Buckle of the Bible Belt" (the Protestant buckle anyway) with seminaries, 700 churches and several of the nation's largest Christian music and publishing company headquarters. Since the Gulf War, Nashville has become home to 11,000 Kurdish immigrants, Kurdistan being the region occupying northern Iraq,

Syria and southeastern Turkey, the result being that Nashville has also inherited the nickname "Little Kurdistan."

What a mix – country music, universities and seminaries, churches, publishing and Little Kurdistan. You get it all in Nashville.

We set up the tent and our camp about half a mile south of the Ryman. It was winter and snow came early. Within days the campsite was a sea of mud and continued to be so for the duration of our Nashville event.

We walked downtown every day; shared with an amazing mix of people mostly on lower Broadway near the honkytonks and massage parlors and even rubbed shoulders with a few country music stars. On Friday nights some of us would hang around the Ryman until the crowd dismissed from the Opry and we'd hand out invitations to the meetings as they left for home.

Word spread among the Opry musicians and stars and it didn't take long before some of them started showing at our tent meetings – Marty Robbins' wife came and played organ for us; Jeannie C. Reilly's bass player Mike joined the party and Skeeter Davis made the mistake of venturing into our midst. Skeeter ended up re-dedicating her life to Christ on one of the nights; her drummer Jimmie and bass player, David, came next and were regular attendees from then on. Skeeter invited us backstage at the

Opry on different occasions and we had the opportunity to meet Bill Monroe, Buck Owens and Marty Robbins.

Mike, the bass player, found Christ and joined with us when we departed Nashville. We toured with Skeeter the following year, coast to coast, her band and our band, the Joyful Noise, as her opening act.

One Friday night, after the Opry let out, Bill and I ran into Marty Robbins on the front steps. He was signing autographs and talking with folks. He knew who we were; his wife had been trying to get him to come to the meetings, but he'd resisted – a lapsed Southern Baptist.

"Marty, we've been praying for you, man. Hope to see you out some night."

"I know, I know," he smiled gentle and friendly. "I need to get with it, don't I?"

We never saw Marty at the meetings. He had heart problems and passed away in December 1982 at the age of 57. I do hope Marty got with it.

Nashville had a new mall so we decided to try it out and ended up in jail for a spell. Same situation, same results – out on O.R. and scolded but there was really nothing anyone could do. A local lawyer, Jack Thompson, represented us during the legal fiasco. He also came to know Christ at the meetings, and often agonized over what we were doing; always torn between his knowledge of the law, his respect for keeping the law and then having to represent a bunch of freaks in a court of law for trespassing at the local mall even though we all knew that we'd broken no laws. Still, his courage in standing with us in those days was nothing short of a miracle.

Chapter 15
The Scandinavian Call

Bill, our leader, had been to Sweden before as part of a Full Gospel Businessmen's junket. He knew people and churches in Sweden and had been looking for ways to begin some version of what we were doing here over there. The opportunity came during our winter in Nashville. The FGB president of Sweden invited Bill back for a tour of Sweden only this time with our band, The Joyful Noise. The tour was arranged, flyers were posted and newspapers were notified that the FAMOUS ROCK BAND FROM AMERICA, The Joyful Noise, was invading Sweden.

In 1973 if you had long hair, played rock music, possessed certain American-made musical instruments unobtainable in Sweden, you automatically qualified as audience-worthy especially among teenagers and twenty-somethings. We flew into Copenhagen, were met there by a wonderful, smiling Swede named Sven Petersson who happened to own a bus he'd used specifically to smuggle Bibles into Yugoslavia; he'd also brought a second bus, an older Scania diesel which had been used as a city bus before being recruited for our purposes. We loaded the gear, the band and Bill into the buses and off we went to Sweden.

From Malmö to Kiruna, Gothenburg to Stockholm we played in churches, schools and public plazas - Joyful Noise rock and then Evangelist Bill (now growing his hair long) preaching to the crowds through our Swedish interpreter. It was like being on tour in the U.S. only for us it was crowds of adoring fans who had no clue who we were.

Memories from that trip are very special. It was the first time in a foreign country for us. The food, the culture, the language, the clothes, the roads, the cars, the religion and spiritual climate put the "foreign" in foreign country. To be received with enthusiasm, to enjoy the absolute focused attention from the audience, to see the responses from old and young to the preaching and testimonies – it was very different from what we'd experienced in the States. Whereas we had regularly encountered resistance, indifference and jail time, we were now overnight best friends with a whole culture. (It seemed like it anyway.)

In one Baptist church, in a very conservative city on the northeastern shores of the Baltic Sea, Luleå (loo' lee oh) or Piteå (Pee' tee oh - can't remember which), the very quiet pastor introduced the band to polite applause in the main sanctuary in front of maybe fifty people. We began to play, but Evangelist Bill, his interpreter and a couple other members of the team sitting on the front pews began pointing and laughing, hands covering mouths. After the first couple songs I was becoming more distracted because the laughing kept coming with our interpreter joining in. I leaned over to Bill asking what was going on –

"Bubba's pants are unzipped," he said and couldn't hold it any more. Bubba Poythress had joined us in Las Vegas and immediately became part of our musical team. Bubba was a recording session player, one of the most accomplished and creative guitarists I've ever known. He had played on records and in concerts for the likes of Bobby Darin, Tina Turner and many others.

And the color in his music played out in his personality and demeanor. Bubba was in every sense of the word an eccentric – about 5'6", long curly hair complimenting a long curly beard and moustache that swallowed up his mouth and bright blue eyes that altered states from mischievous twinkle, to steely concentration to Never Never Land all in the space of twenty seconds. Give him a leather vest and a sword and he would have been a perfect dwarf in The Hobbit. Bubba opened up conversations as if you already knew what he was talking about: "Hey, it's coming in from the east today. Watch your back," which could have been a reference to last night's sermon or the weather or new lyrics to a song. If your response was a look of confusion, he'd just start laughing and walk off.

We learned early not to worry when we saw Bubba carrying his rubber enema bottle around camp. Enemas were part of his daily routine. And we never knew what to expect in a recording studio – he came up with the strangest ideas. Once in Nashville he kept hearing chimes in a song but didn't like the sound of the concert grand piano, which was the only instrument in the studio that was even close to a chime. It wasn't long before we looked out at the grand and Bubba was hunched over the sounding board tapping away with a screwdriver on individual strings. He kept at it until he found the melody line he was looking for, showed it to Mark and that became the perfect chime sound on the record. Genius.

So there was poor Bubba, up in front of the church, pants unzipped and laughter beginning to build from the front row. Snickers gave way to full on bellows, and, fearing cataclysm, I leaned over to Bubba and told him the problem; Bubba with straight face, turned to the back wall, zipped up, turned back, continued playing and the entire band broke down in hysterics. Older Swedish women turned to one another in confusion; men tried to keep a straight face; kids laughed with us; Lynn, our female drummer, fell off her drum stool laughing, peed her pants and had to run off the stage to the ladies' room. It was out of control. Bill grabbed the microphone and tried explaining through his interpreter that we were simply experiencing the Holy Spirit and that "we're always this way!" But then he realized what he'd just said which only triggered another 15 minutes of the same. It was hopeless. We did find out later that many of those attending that night had actually been very touched and blessed in spite of the outbreak.

From Piteå and Luleå we continued to head north along the E10 and ended up above the Arctic Circle in Kiruna, the steel mining center of Sweden. We discovered that Kiruna, located in one of the bleakest parts of northern Europe, is the largest municipality in Sweden, almost 19,500 square kilometers. Americans know this area of Scandinavia as Lapland but the native people there are called Sami, and yes, they still herd reindeer and no, Lapland is not a term they use, since Lapps are more native to Finland.

The Samis knew about the iron ore deposits for centuries; and Swedes discovered them in the 1700s and 1800s, but there was no means of transporting the ore from north to south until the first railroad in the late 1800s. Now it is a massive underground mine with two-lane tunnels and semi-size ore trucks driving around half a mile below the surface.

We had been invited to play for the miners through the local state church (Lutheran) in Kiruna. So we agreed to go and the experience was amazing. It was late October 1974 and winter had already set in – so cold that diesel fuel anti-freeze was required in the bus and our American parkas did little to insulate us against the below-zero chill.

Upon our arrival at the mine, the band equipment and people were loaded onto a small ore train; we entered the mine and offloaded again when we arrived at the elevators. It was at that point that we descended a half-mile down, loaded another ore train and moved everything into a cafeteria area, set up drums, guitars and microphones and proceeded to give the lunching miners a concert.

We learned later that almost all of the men were Communists and that religion played only a marginal role in the life and culture of Kiruna. We received some polite applause but mostly hoots from the miners, loaded up the gear and headed up the half-mile shaft; set up and played again in the surface version of the cafeteria to the cafeteria office staff and went on our way.

Today I still think about it – a half-mile down; miles above the Arctic Circle; winter; Communists. How, what, why? I can't wait to see the replay.

There were many more concerts in many more churches, including some in Denmark, and we headed back home. But this first overseas trip started something brewing in our hearts and minds; and we knew this would not be the last time.

Chapter 16
A Fast Turnaround

It didn't take long at all. We caught the whiff of
change and challenge in the air and immediately
began making plans for Europe. Christ is the
Answer was about to go global. We prayed for
guidance, fifty of us were selected, and I was chosen
to be the team leader. I do not know why; never
have, but there it was. I even wondered if being the
team leader on the first expedition into unknown
waters meant I was the most dispensable; the
hapless guide in the opening scenes of Raiders of
the Lost Ark: "Let's throw 'im out there, George; see
if he swims."

We took some time in Weldon to learn a few
Swedish phrases; Bill contacted Christian
Broadcasting Network in Virginia and they donated
a new tent; we put it on a steamer to Gothenburg,
Sweden; bought our tickets and said good-bye to
America. We had our first meeting on a paved
parking lot near Gothenburg central in June 1973.

Again, we were pleasantly surprised by the response
of the Swedes – no indifference; they either loved
you or hated you. If they believed in God, they'd say
so; if they didn't they'd say so – either way, you
always knew where a Swede stood regarding his
spiritual orientation. At one point we played a
concert in a large state church in the north, and I
approached a tall, well-dressed gentleman who had
listened to the music and the preaching of evangelist

Bill. He was lingering around for some reason. I introduced myself; we began a conversation (most Swedes are very fluent in English), which led to his volunteering that he'd been a member of this church since childhood.

"Oh," I asked, "so you've been a Christian that long as well?"

"No, of course not," he said. "I'm just a church member in this old place (almost apologetic in tone). But I liked what you had to say, and I will think about it."

I was somewhat dazed: "of course not?" I'd not heard that from one single American ... ever. I didn't know how to respond to him because I hadn't experienced that kind of no bull honesty. I suppose I nodded and mumbled something about praying for him. That's what I mean by the honesty we encountered, and not just in Sweden, but pretty much everywhere in Europe. It was refreshing on so many different levels.

During the meetings in Gothenburg we were, of course, approaching and speaking with people on the streets. There were very few malls in Europe; most commerce carried on as it had for centuries in the urban areas; access to people was a piece of cake compared to the U.S. So there we were in downtown Gothenburg when what should arrive in the massive harbor but the very first Russian battleship to ever visit a Swedish harbor; a goodwill gesture between Sweden and Russia we found out, during the Cold War years of the 'Sixties and 'Seventies.

Sailors and officers were given shore leave in order to sample the Western, bourgeois decadence now at their fingertips, and they came on shore in droves but carefully monitored in groups of four, each with a senior Soviet officer as chaperone in case the decadence started going to their heads.

And we met them with our Bibles and invitations not knowing quite how to speak with them – we didn't speak Russian and they didn't speak English, so it was hand gestures and smiles. Once the senior officer caught our scent, he would shuffle off his brood to the nearest hot dog stand or porno shop.

But one day, two of our guys, Jerry and B.J., happened to run into the captain of the ship while downtown and spoke with him (broken English) and, before spilling the beans as to who they were and Who they represented, managed to let him know that they were the personal road managers of a VERY FAMOUS AMERICAN ROCK BAND called the Joyful Noise.

And he asked, "Like the Rolling Stones?"

To which they replied, "Absolutely."

Which led to, "Would your band do a concert on our ship for the sailors?"

To which they replied, "Absolutely." And then they beat it back to the tent and told us what was about to go down.

Long story short, we moved all of the band equipment from the tent to the dock the very next Sunday morning (yes, a Sunday morning rock concert), the captain and crew met us at the bottom of the gangplank; greeted us like royalty and a team of sailors helped us get the equipment to the aft deck of the ship. One of the officers noticed that he'd already seen some of the Americans who accompanied us to the docks – "Weren't they out and about downtown talking with our people?"

To which I replied, "I don't think so. You must have them confused with some other long-haired Americans who we've also heard are in town." - a profile in courage.

That Sunday morning, eight hundred Russian sailors and officers gathered on that deck under a giant tarpaulin spread out for the occasion, officers in the front row and sailors squeezed into every other available space, all eyes aft and ears fully prepared for deafening volume.

I was chosen as the official spokesperson for the band, so the interpreter (an officer) asked me how he should introduce us and what would be the theme of our concert this morning? He followed quickly with, "Please do not speak about God at this gathering. It is against our ship policy," so I knew something was up and that someone on board was wise to our sneaky scheme.

I assured him that nothing about God would be said or sung about during the concert (I lied) and insisted that the main theme of the morning would be love, and would that be okay to sing about which, given the stalemate between two nuclear-armed adversaries, seemed like a good idea since I was the American on his Russian battleship. He said it would be okay, and we proceeded.

I leaned over to the band members after my conversation with the interpreter and called an audible: "No one use the word "Jesus" or "God", ok? I'll explain later. If we do, they may shut down the concert."

We mumbled through our repertoire when it came to God references but at the end, as we were preparing to sing "Praise Ye the Lord All Ye Nations," I felt compelled to explain to the men that, yes, they'd met some of us on the streets of Gothenburg and that yes, this great love we've been singing about this morning has a source; and we think that Source is pretty cool and we think you may know what we're talking about, so thanks again for having us this morning. And then we started the song before anyone could stop us. During the intro, the senior officers in the front row began whispering to one another and pointing upward – "Bogo!" they said; Bogo in Russian meaning "God."

We finished the concert to cheers from the sailors and polite applause from the officers, and the team of men who'd helped us carry everything up the gangplank carried it back down to our waiting trucks. As we stood dockside, one tall sailor pulled me aside:

"Can I speak with you for one short minute?" he asked in very broken English. "Thank you so much for coming today to sing about God. I am Christian and my family back in Russia is Christian. Please keep us in your prayers. I cannot speak about God here or they will make my family suffer back home." And then he pulled off the metal pin attached to the front of his winter hat and gave it to me. It had the hammer and sickle emblazoned on the front.

"When you see this you'll pray for me, right?"

I nodded and said, "Absolutely, brother."

We looked up and the entire dockside of the battleship was lined with Russian sailors waving at us, shouting thanks and throwing us various pins and medallions to remember them. Amazing.

After everything was packed away in the trucks, the officers brought us back on board the ship for a tour. We'd known ahead of time that there would be a tour of the ship, so we managed to find some Russian New Testaments. Each of us stuffed a few in our pants and coat pockets prior to re-boarding the ship. During the tour, they brought us to the sailors' living quarters; we'd wait for the right moment and quickly stuff a New Testament under a pillow here and there. We had copies of our record as well which also went on board that ship.

Ever since then, I've gained a whole new understanding of what it means: "What God opens, no one can shut, and what he shuts no one can open." (Revelations 3:7)

Chapter 17
Amsterdam

From Gothenburg the tent, trucks and people
headed east, across the Baltic and on to Helsinki,
Finland and, after that, a short stay in Lahti near the
Russian border. Until that time we'd never been in
a place where literally nothing could be understood
of the language. Finnish is a derivative of the Uralic
languages (Finnish, Hungarian and Estonian) along
with a touch of Sami (Lapland) to boot. Finland is
"Suomi" in the Finnish language. Jesus was Jesus
fortunately, and that was about the extent of any
similarity.

Our time in Finland was wonderful; the people were
wonderful and generous; gentle and very receptive
to our unorthodox presentation of the gospel. It was
1974; they lived in the shadow of the Russian bear.
They'd known his power; they'd been occupied and
danced to his pipes. They knew the sweet breath of
freedom and did not hesitate to take advantage of
assembling in public in Christ's name in order to
worship together.

The tent was literally packed with Finns every night.
The meetings began at 7:30 but the tent would
remain vacant until 7:25. Within five minutes, it
filled up – amazing. The opening night in Helsinki
was a bit humbling for me. I was leading worship
and at 7:29, guitar in hand, I was setting the dials
one last time on my guitar amplifier before
beginning. The stage was built in two tiers, the

amps being on the back elevated tier and the microphones situated on the lower tier toward the front.

I was excited to see all of the people and decided to express my excitement by jumping, not stepping, from tier two to tier one on my way to the microphone in order to get the service started. My feet hit the tier one floor and just kept going, down, down, down to the earth four feet below. On my way through the stage the neck of the guitar snapped off and I was left standing with only my chest and head showing. My shins were scraped and bleeding as was my self-confidence. The guitar was in ruins; a very expensive Gibson guitar that had belonged to Bubba. Turns out the stage floor had been made from some very flimsy particleboard and did not have sufficient support to carry my weight.

A gasp went up from the audience; the guys in the band helped me out of the three-foot-wide hole I'd made in the stage and the show went on: "No worries, everyone. I'm fine. Let's worship God." Uh huh. I haven't forgotten that night, obviously, and Bubba, during a recent phone call, let me know that now, 38 years later, he was beginning to find forgiveness in his heart.

Our spies were sent ahead from Helsinki to Amsterdam to scout a good location for the tent community. Meetings concluded in Lahti, the trucks and buses rumbled southwest back through

Sweden, south into Denmark and southwest again through the northern tip of Germany into the Netherlands. We managed to find a nice block of land within the city limits, small miracle, and began working the surrounding urban neighborhoods advertising the meetings.

At that time, the Netherlands, and particularly Amsterdam, were taking progressive thinking to its limits and a bit beyond. Marijuana use was and is legal. Prostitution was and is legal save for street walking, which, of course, is well beyond the pale. Coffee shops were also pot shops (hence coffee pots) and young people we encountered in certain downtown areas openly shot up heroin and sniffed glue. The downtown post office was a fave place for drug deals and its floors were often occupied with kids sleeping off the previous night's high or laying in a glue-induced stupor.

We were not ready for this – a cornucopia of the flesh that our Midwest-raised, babe-like brains could not absorb or understand. We'd experienced drugs and participated in the sins of the flesh, but always in the dark; we'd experimented, but this? Shopping for a prostitute in a shop window? This was not experimentation for these people; it was a lifestyle.

We changed street tactics and began going out at night after our meetings. De Wallen, the red-light district, forty square blocks of it, didn't really start cranking until 11 pm so it didn't make sense to go earlier. We took up positions at different places along the narrow, cobblestone streets, Bibles and meeting invitations in hand, and began talking with passersby.

We encountered resistance almost immediately ... from the young ladies in the windows. No, they were not interested in what we had to say and yes, get your ass away from my window. We learned to scoot slightly to the side so we wouldn't block the way in or out or obstruct the eyes of the shoppers. When the warnings of the ladies failed to move us out, we were then confronted by the pimps who ran the shop district syndicates for both drugs and prostitution. The pimps were considerably less patient or understanding. Verbal threats led to pushing, which led to both male and female members of our tribe being launched into the canals which circulate all through this historic district.

There were four major canals built during Amsterdam's golden years (17th century) when it was the world's largest and richest port city (The Dutch East India Company established the world's first stock exchange in 1602, trading their own shares). The canals were built in four concentric half circles with earthen dams or dikes piled on either side to both contain the canals and to provide a solid landfill for buildings and streets. The names, House of Lords Canal, Emperor's Canal, Prince's Canal and the outer Singel Canal, were not familiar to us, but we were introduced by way of baptism. I'm not sure what the current condition of the water is, but at that time (1974) the canals (now a national landmark) were full of sewage and chemical waste. One night one of our guys was carrying a large cross through the District. He was caught, beaten up, and he and the cross were thrown into the canal. The police were always notified when one of us was thrown in and it was SOP for them to take us in a squad car to the local health office for cleansing and shots.

Three weeks into our stay, a couple of our men were summoned to the police chief's office. We'd been warned out of there by police patrols (the police never entered De Wallen unless absolutely necessary; apparently De Wallen's pimps policed themselves) and the captain echoed, "You are not safe down there. They will continue to throw you in those canals, beat you up and kill you, if necessary. This is a legal commerce in Amsterdam and they will enforce their rights (apparently murder included). If you continue to go down there we will not guarantee your safety."

He also mentioned that in our two weeks we'd managed to shut down 70% of the red light business. People were not comfortable with us near the shop windows, smiling, sporting Bibles and reminding them that God loved them. How do you shut down that much business just doing that? I found this hard to believe but we stayed for the sake of the 30% who's appetite for what the district offered remained undiminished. We owed them that.

The chief's warning was prophetic – that night all hell broke loose; a gang of pimps, some armed with billy clubs and brass knuckles, attacked wherever they could find us. Many were beaten or thrown in the canals or both. One of the guys on our team was on the wrong end of a set of brass knuckles and his face was concaved which ended in a trip to the hospital. The damage was so extensive that the upper half of his face had to be placed in a bright white, plaster cast. We made national Dutch news and his Phantom-of-the-opera-like face cast with his long red hair sticking out was the highlight on TV and in the papers. The media loved us.

The next thing that happened that night – two pimps accosted one of our girls. They threatened to throw her and one of the guys (we sent one man with one woman as a precaution) into the canal as well. Our couple noticed a police car a block away, and backed up toward it, beckoning to the officer in the squad for help. He saw them, got back in his car and left the scene. Linda proceeded to face the two pimps and, with a holy boldness that was actually common for her, she began to rebuke them both. "Who do you think you are trying to intimidate me? I'm just a little thing and you're so big." And then to their surprise she began shouting, "I rebuke you both in the name of Jesus! Satan, take your hands off these two men so they might hear the gospel and be saved!" They stopped dead in their tracks and took off; no mere tourist she.

Churches in Amsterdam joined the chief of police in condemning our foolishness and many threatened to withdraw from attending our meetings. Their argument was that we were ruining their testimony in Amsterdam by being in the District at all, to which we replied, "What testimony?"

The Salvation Army was the exception; they went down with us and, we learned, had already conducted "salvation marches" through the red-lit alleyways. They were also one of the few Christian ministries living near and ministering in De Wallen, knowing its well-kept secret: in spite of the frivolity and attraction, De Wallen chewed up and spit out its denizens on a regular basis. Where do you go when your veins collapse and you're racked with disease and you look forty-going-on-sixty and are no longer useful to Joe the pimp? You got it, the Salvation Army coffee shop.

We discovered after we'd been gone from there for a few months that a handful of prostitutes who'd come to Christ around that time began their own coffee house and hostel for recovering women who had no place else to go. As of 2008 the Dutch Ministry of Justice ordered the closing of 320 out of the 400 window shops in Amsterdam citing that they had become a cesspool of drugs and human trafficking and no longer reflected the values of the city; what we might call - insight.

And Joe the pimp, (real person), came to our tent meeting one night ... with a gun. Joe was the epitome of a UFC fighter - muscular, mean and a life-long street thug, pimp and drug runner; a Kirk Douglas lookalike with steel blue eyes and a smile that reminded you of a hungry shark. He ruled in the red light and he'd had it with our invasion. "Find the leader and take him out" seemed to be his strategy just as it had been with the assassin in Phoenix, Arizona.

As the music played he hung out at the back of the big top, and Leo Ramos walked over and began to chat. Leo, you'll remember, was our street-smart, tag-along, former Army-sergeant-in- Viet Nam, mafia hit man: that Leo ... began to chat up Joe-with-a-gun and, as the music and preaching went on and as Joe-with-a-gun and Leo talked, something attached itself to Joe's heart, he began trying too hard to force back tears and ended up making his way to the front with Leo, not to kill but to pray. Joe joined our band of merry men and made it to Italy with us before returning to Amsterdam.

In 2007 Amsterdam placed a bronze sculpture by artist Els Rijerse named "Belle" in the Oude Kerk plaza (Old Church) on one of the main streets in De Wallen. The inscription on the plaque under Belle says, "Respect sex workers all over the world." The oldest building and church in Amsterdam became a Dutch Reformed Church in 1578. And now this church plaza contains this sculpture and is ringed by shop windows containing Belle's real-life sisters-in-trade. I'm not sure what to think about that. The famous missionary, C.T. Studd once wrote,

Some wish to live within the sound
Of church or chapel bell.
I want to run a rescue shop
Within a yard of hell.

C.T. would have gotten his wish on this one. And I think about the ghost of John Calvin hovering nearby, watching this parade in front of his church in the heart of Amsterdam, brooding over his own words:

"The whole world is a theater for the display of the divine goodness, wisdom, justice, and power, but the Church is the orchestra, as it were—the most conspicuous part of it."

What do you think about this, Mr. Calvin?

A few years later, we would have similar confrontations with streetwalkers in Milan, Italy. The ladies of the night in Milan were often not actually ladies, but transvestites and transsexuals. Our tent site in Milan happened to be located on a street they considered their turf. There was immediate conflict. We walked along the street at night trying to speak with them about Christ, and they walked into our camp night and day to intimidate or tempt. It was a moral and spiritual circus.

The team leader by that time was Basil Hairgrove, an ex-school teacher from San Antonio, Texas. The streetwalkers knew that Basil was the team leader, and he soon earned the nickname "Mr. Basil."

"Hallo, yoo hoo, Mr. Basil!" they would call out from across the street. "Are you coming to see us tonight?" Or they might wander into camp after everyone was in bed, "Is Mr. Basil here?" they would ask the night guards. "We'd lo-o-o-o-ve to see Mr. Basil!" Italian TV learned about this and Mr. Basil was on the evening news.

Hilarious ... for awhile, until it wasn't hilarious anymore, because Mr. Basil and group were beginning to put a dent in their business. Picture Iris or Betty, six foot two inches, high heels, very revealing street garb, no undergarments, trying to flag down his/her next customer; the customer stops and one of our guys or girls, standing close behind Betty, says something about God to the customer. Betty is leaning in through the car window trying to make her/his deal and she/he is not amused. The nervous customer drives off without Betty because he's afraid of being busted. Multiply that scene enough times and tempers began to flare.

The first incident involved one of the transvestites jumping in his car after seeing Basil trespassing on the sidewalk clearly designated "Transvestites Only" and heading straight for Mr. Basil full throttle - car screaming down the SIDEWALK! Basil avoided being run over by jumping onto a retaining wall. Next night shots rang out and bullets started flying through our camp, one from a shooter in an apartment across the street and another from a transvestite toting a gun shooting from an open position on the sidewalk. No one was hurt, and we did not stop or leave. The police were called and did absolutely nothing.

Other streetwalkers, sensing that we weren't leaving, would walk into camp, sit down and have coffee before going to work that night. We were never quite sure what to expect, and we never learned what impact, if any, we had on their spiritual lives. It was just a really weird crossroads we hit in Milan where Spirit intersected flesh trade. We learned over the years that whenever this happened in whatever venue, there was almost always violence enacted toward us (witness Amsterdam, Phoenix, Gothenburg) ... zero tolerance for light in a very dark place.

Chapter 18
Passage to Italy by Way of Austria and Yugoslavia

We'd been to Vienna before, as part of an earlier excursion of The Joyful Noise. Vienna, the City of Music, had been hospitable. The band played in schools, churches, discos, on the streets and in the subway tunnels.

It was quirky how it had taken place; Harald Bredesen, former Dutch Reformed pastor and Christian television personality in the '70s, accompanied us during our swing through Germany, Austria and Yugoslavia. He had never seen anything like it but was thrilled to tag along just for the sheer excitement of watching impossible doors open in front of us with little to no forethought or planning.

We began our first Viennese tour on the street corners serenading passersby with our strange little Jesus songs. Mark played banjo, I strummed an acoustic guitar and Debbie and Gayle sang. People stopped to listen mostly because they'd never seen or heard anything like us: a Puerto Rican, left-handed banjo player; two attractive young ladies in granny gowns and a hippie strumming along; and we played country and blue-grass and sang about God ... and we were Americans. It was too much for folks to pass up, apparently, so they stood and watched and listened and went on their way.

Harald watched the watchers; he was irrepressibly joyous and embarrassingly spontaneous. No one was off limits as a potential conversation partner for Harald, and his joy and innocence would overflow onto the listener and pull them in. "Hear ye, hear ye, step right up!!!"

One day an unexpected visitor did step up; a tall, lanky Viennese with (I am not kidding) a bowler, a monocle, a moustache, a long, dark trench coat and an umbrella/cane (straight out of character casting for 101 Dalmatians or The Pink Panther). He stood next to Harald for at least a half hour intrigued by our music, magnetized to the spot by Harald's amazing banter. The man (I think his name was Klaus) finally identified himself to Harald as the president of the largest talent/booking agency in Vienna responsible for booking all live music into all of Vienna's vibrant and numerous discotheques. He mentioned to Harald in passing: "It's a shame these guys don't have band equipment (he was witnessing the street version of the Joyful Noise); I could book them into every discotheque in town. I love this."

Harald's jaw dropped: "You happen to be in luck! They have all of their instruments, drums, electric guitars, keyboards – everything; here in Vienna with them!" Harald, the booking agent and promotions specialist.

That night we played in our first discotheque, the Voom Voom, in the heart of Vienna, and several other discos thereafter. We shared the stage in a battle of the bands one night with a Czech progressive rock group. We talked and prayed with kids (including the members of the Czech band) into the wee hours at each gig. Spiritual hunger was palpable, but church had become irrelevant; an old, stodgy thing that spoke nothing into their lives. But an American rock band, that was different; it was on their level and they responded.

Chapter 19
Bibles for Yugoslavia

By 1973 the Catholic Charismatic movement had spread throughout Europe and two of Austria's prominent Catholic Charismatics (Ernst Florian and Johanna Winter) lived just forty miles south of Vienna. Harald was still traveling with us and knew the family through his television connections, and one phone call later we headed south for Katzelsdorf. The Winters lived in a castle (Schloss Eichbüchel) on the side of a hill overlooking the valley west of Katzelsdorf. Mrs. Winter was, literally, Johanna, the youngest of the Von Trapp family daughters, the family upon whom The Sound of Music was based. The Winter castle where we were to stay was not the original Von Trapp family castle, but Schloss Eichbüchel had a history all its own being the location of what became known as the "Eichbüchler-Gespräche," an Austrian/American think tank started by Winter and the "birthplace of the (modern) republic of Austria" shortly after World War II. Henry Kissinger is among former and present diplomats who participated in these political seminars at the castle.

The Winters treated us as honored guests; Johanna fixed an amazing meal, made sure we had adequate housing in the upstairs bedrooms and next day sent us into the garden to pull weeds and harvest potatoes!! Awesome!

Schloss Eichbüchel was also where we began hatching our first plot to smuggle Bibles into Yugoslavia. As I mentioned earlier, our bus driver, Sven, had outfitted his bus for the specific purpose of smuggling large numbers of Bibles into Eastern bloc countries where Bibles were forbidden. Sven had worked for Open Doors, a ministry founded by Brother Andrew (we never knew his last name), and had experience in this sort of thing, so we felt confident in his knowledge and experience. We also had a contact, a Pentecostal pastor in Zagreb, not far from the Yugoslav border with Austria, who knew people who knew people – like that; a very clandestine, carefully-thought-out system whereby Bibles could be taken across the border into a monastery in Ljubljana and then distributed to the Christian church throughout Yugoslavia from there.

Which is what we did ... plans were made, phone calls completed and stacks of Slovenian and Croatian Bibles, brought along from Amsterdam, were carefully hidden in special compartments Sven had constructed behind paneling and flooring in the bus.

Our destination was a monastery in Ljubljana where Catholic brothers and church members met for prayer. The monastery was located on the outskirts of the city and the meetings were never advertised, the Yugoslav government being Communist-controlled. And so began our first trip behind the Iron Curtain into Yugoslavia: two Swedish buses lugging all our band equipment and the Bibles.

We crossed the border and headed for Ljubljana toward evening. At the border of Yugoslavia and Austria, Sven cautioned us to remain cool and to act natural (he never did mention the length of prison sentences involved with smuggling contraband, I suspect, on purpose!). The Slavic Bibles were stashed everywhere, and, having done this before; he knew it wouldn't take much to arouse suspicion. As we pulled up to the border station, our first visitor was the main man himself, an older, somewhat rotund gentleman with a full face and a grey military buzz cut, dressed in an olive green customs uniform complete with officer's dress hat and a very stern look. Just prior to his boarding the bus, Mark had a brainstorm. He pulled out his banjo, I pulled out my guitar, and we began to sing blue grass: first, "You get a line, I'll get a pole, honey!" and then good old blue grass gospel – "Farther along we'll … know more about it …". The guard listened and began to smile; and he loved it and began dancing and hopping and turning up and down the aisle of the bus, as we clapped and sang and cheered him on. After four or five minutes of that, he had forgotten to search us, turned at the front of the bus, gave a big smile and cheer and waved us on through. It was hilarious.

Chapter 20
Contra Communist – Lawbreakers and Yankee Scoundrels

We delivered the Bibles that night to the monastery in Ljubljana. I remember sitting out in the bus in the dark as Sven went inside and spoke with the monastery brothers about how the Bible transfer would proceed. I felt disoriented and apprehensive. It was the dead of night, dense rural darkness, everyone whispering, waiting, and all of us knowing we were doing something totally against Yugoslavian law. The aforementioned Brother Andrew, who was well acquainted with this sort of thing, wrote a book entitled The Ethics of Smuggling ... A WHOLE BOOK! ... Addressed to, believe it or not, the believing Christian world because, as it happened, his biggest critics were not Communist governments but well-meaning evangelical Christians:

"How can you justify breaking a country's laws just for the sake of getting Bibles through its borders?"

"Doesn't your conscience bother you that you're lying to these people?"

"I'm sorry, we cannot support what you're doing. The Bible says that we are to honor the king and those in authority."

Blah, blah, blah ...

Hence, his book: a well-thought-out apologetic on why it is not only right, but necessary to take Bibles into places that do not allow them – something about God's law superseding men's laws. And there we were, waiting for a possible swooping upon by the authorities, openly and wantonly transgressing a hundred different laws and codes put in place by a government ruled and run on the premise that the State determines what you may or may not believe in and how you may act that out. We figured it was at least 50/50 as to whether we were acting ethically or lawfully and decided we'd take our chances; that we would get these Bibles to hungry hearts and famished souls, thirsting for any nourishment in a dark and hellish culture.

Once we had the green light, the Bibles were taken inside the monastery and we made ourselves at home in a wonderful, beautiful room with candles and warmth and praying men of God; worship and prayer with the dear brothers and a peaceful night on the monastery floor in our sleeping bags.

After breakfast, we loaded up and headed back north to the Austrian border, and during the drive, Sven and I wondered if a short stop off in a border city on the Yugoslav side might not be in order. We knew Yugoslavia was Communist-controlled, but how far would they allow us to test their limits of tolerance? So we settled on the idea of stopping in Maribor, just a few miles from Austria, and conducting a one-hour gospel raid and then beating it for the border.

Although we were out of Bibles, we still had a number of gospel leaflets and pamphlets in various Slavic languages – enough to keep our small group busy for an hour. And so the bus pulled up near the city center, we synchronized our watches and agreed to meet back at the bus in 60 minutes. Sven and I hung out at the bus in case of trouble.

We didn't have to wait long ... for trouble. A few of the group began passing out literature in the city square. Within five minutes plain clothes policemen showed up, identified themselves to us and politely but firmly escorted the lawbreakers back to the bus. Those who'd been busted stayed with us in the bus while the cops lit up cigarettes and waited for the rest.

Surprisingly, most of the team members were not caught. Instead, they came back without their literature, amazed at the hunger for information about God in the hearts of the people they encountered on the streets. My wife and another girl with us, Karen, happened into a school. Instead of going to ask permission from the principal, they simply began walking through the halls, handing out literature to students and teachers. The response was incredible. Such hunger. It lasted only a few minutes, and they, too, were confronted and escorted back to the bus by police.

And so we tested the system, and it worked ... their system, I mean. We were shown the way to the border and invited to please leave. Once again the liberty of these poor people had been crushed and their access to their one hope denied. It was a sobering reminder to us, in the midst of global Cold War tensions, that the Communist system was alive and well, and we believers were not welcome.

But I do believe that our system also worked; that system whereby followers in the Way of Jesus respond to His orders to go wherever, whenever so that others might hear, or in this case, read, about Him. In retrospect, ours was the superior system: irresistible, irrefutable and, yes, irritating; but absolutely efficient and powerful. As it had been on the Russian battleship, so it was also on the streets of Maribor, Slovenia: guaranteed success because we tried.

Chapter 21
Passing Passau

I've been on a small detour in the last two chapters, the trip to Austria and Yugoslavia happening on a timeline of its own, but in the general vicinity of our adventures in Amsterdam.

We set as our next tent meeting destination beautiful Vienna; and why not – we'd visited once already with the Joyful Noise and had received a wonderful welcome. So the happy troupe took off from Amsterdam on the Amstel to Vienna on the Danube – four trucks, by this time and two buses along with a couple cars.

From Amsterdam we headed south through Germany with our European version of the American Christ is the Answer caravan and arrived in Munich. We staged three vehicles there for a few days and sent envoys ahead to Vienna to find a tent site and secure permission to enter the country. The Munich staging area came about because a German pastor driving along side our caravan on the E52 ring around the north side of the city saw the Christ is the Answer (in huge English letters) on the side of our trucks and started waving and honking wildly as he drew even with me in the lead truck. I waved back, but continued on. "We got a caravan here on the autobahn buddy; stop bothering me!" He refused to stop waving and honking, so I knew we either had something really wrong at the back end of the truck or he was desperate in some way. We pulled over, all eight vehicles, on the German autobahn, cars and semis racing past, all competing for a Grand Prix pole position. It is very difficult to describe the speed at which things happen on the autobahn but for most American drivers, you'd need diapers.

Klaus Puplichhuisen (poop' – lick - hoosen ... don't even go there) ran to the cab of my truck, hopped onto the step and leaned his head in and began an up-close-and-personal conversation, which was the last thing in the world I expected from a German, the inventors and personification of Stoic.

"Who are you guys, where did you come from, I've never heard of you, are you really preaching on the streets, I preach on the streets, too, at the university every week, so can't you stop here for a few days and preach with me and then meetings at my Catholic charismatic group and I'll find food for you and a place to park your trucks and I can't believe this, I can't believe this, WOW!"

Klaus was, as it turned out, the number one interpreter used in Germany by all of the great American evangelists: Billy Graham, Luis Palau, etc. and was known everywhere by the German evangelical community. And he was good as gold on his word: within two hours the trucks were parked in an unused lot, a place for sleeping and eating was acquired and we were playing and testifying in churches.

In my wildest dreams I had not imagined an interpreter like this man: so fast, so precise, that it was almost like not having an interpreter. He matched my 24-year-old energy, watt for watt, jolt for jolt, smile for smile, holler for holler. It was like preaching with my own German clone, a verbal shadow, a perfect mirror of every gesture and every pause. If you've preached through an interpreter, you will know how rare it is to find a man like this; Klaus, the crazy man from the autobahn.

Munich also became a perfect staging area for our move to Austria. We did not yet have our permits to set up the tent in Vienna; scouting had to be done, a large enough vacant lot located. The report from our scouts was not good. It took much more time than we had expected to locate property and we settled into a dreary wait in Munich.

Finally the time came – the trucks had to be moved, the gypsies needed to be gone, so we headed east for Passau, the crossing point on the border that we felt was small enough that we could inconspicuously pass into Austria with a minimum of trouble. We had been told that Austria was not friendly to efforts like ours and would most likely offer resistance if we attempted a crossing at the primary border near Salzburg.

The bluffs on which this ancient city is built offered beauty and scenery to astound the most jaded traveler. These were the foothills of the Alps, and you could see the Danube River winding through the city at several vantage points along the road. Castles dotted the bluffs ... castles! There were no bad views; it was all gorgeous. It was also the worst place we could have chosen to cross a border.

We had finally secured the tent site in Vienna and authorities in Vienna assured us that there would be no problem at the German border if we just showed them we had the permission letter for the tent in Vienna. That proved not to be true. Basil Hairgrove and his wife, Barbara, our scouts, arrived with the letter, and, upon arriving in Passau, we headed straight for the border post, pulled our trucks, buses and assorted other vehicles to the side and approached immigration.

We showed them our paper work, they made a few phone calls to their superiors and announced their refusal to let us into the country. "You have no money, no food and no permission," they insisted. "How will you support yourselves while you are in the country?" We explained that we lived through the generous support of Christian believers everywhere we went, and that we would be adequately provided for once we got to Vienna.

They made some more phone calls, motioned me into their office and a smallish Austrian captain about sixty years old with a high forehead, a long, thin face accented by a long, thin nose and an icy stare (I learned later that Heir Hitler and his family lived in Passau from 1892-1894 - I think he left his first cousin behind) informed me we would be allowed through only if we could show proof of support: enough money and food in our possession for two weeks, which was the duration of the meetings in Vienna.

We didn't have the money or the food, and we were stuck. A few hundred yards back from this border post was a large grazing field along the highway, and we secured permission from the farmer to park our trucks near there. You have to imagine the scene: 120 men, women and children in long hair, beards, granny gowns, blue jeans and old boots stuck on this German hillside overlooking Passau. Stuck in the mud of a perfect circumstantial storm - not enough money to go backward or forward. Germany didn't want us and Austria didn't want us.

So we did what any self-respecting Jesus gypsy would do: we prayed and then began a bonfire. There was a large stack of old railroad ties in the farmer's field, and he said we could use them for warmth. The next day the Red Cross heard about us and brought out soup and bread. It wasn't long before television stations in Austria, Germany and The Netherlands heard about the 120 "Jesus hippies" camped out in Passau because of the unreasonable Austrian border guards.

We were an overnight news gold mine. For two days news crews with video cameras sat down with us around our railroad tie bonfire, filmed us and interviewed us. Because of our notoriety, money started coming in from all over Germany. People would just drive up to the hillside, walk over with envelopes of money, wish us well and disappear. A businessman in Innsbruck, Austria who owned a cheese factory contacted us and donated all the bread, cheese, sausage and milk we would need for our two-week stay in Vienna.

Within a week we marched back to the border office with two thousand dollars and a truckload full of food. The little captain made another phone call and several hours later announced to us we still could not enter Austria. The national security office in Vienna was now involved, and they wanted a guarantee from Italy, our next destination, that we would be allowed in to Italy after we were finished in Vienna. Of course we knew that no such permission or guarantee even existed in Italy, and the Austrians knew it, too.

I journeyed to Vienna with a German interpreter and Basil. We arranged a meeting with the security minister in charge of the border police. We explained the details of how we had been provided for by the citizenry of Germany and Austria, but he remained unfazed.

"Either get advance permission from Italy, or you do not enter Austria."

Something began to rise up in me in his office. I'm not sure if it was frustration or prophecy, but this was obduracy beyond what my patience could endure. I warned him that he didn't know with whom he was dealing – that God had sent us to Vienna, and if he stopped us, he was hindering what God wanted to do there. He was not impressed and he still refused. "You shall not pass!" We never entered Austria and never had our tent meeting.

One week after we left the Passau border and went to Italy through Switzerland, the Austrian Communist Party used the vacant lot in Vienna to stage a youth rally. One year later, the two border guards responsible for refusing us entry into Austria were both shot to death by a drug runner at the Passau border. We never did set foot in Austria, but we had a great time on that hill overlooking the Danube valley. Each night we sat around the fire, worshipping God, fellowshipping and praying and eating lots of Austrian bread, cheese and sausage. By the end of our stay, the huge pile of railroad ties was gone.

Chapter 22
My Clever Plan

The Austrians didn't want us and we were perched on the German border with nowhere to go – "O, that magic feeling." We had no open doors in Germany, Austrian prospects were gone, but we had felt that Italy would be our next destination after Austria. So this time we sent Basil ahead of us to Italy – Rome, specifically. We gave him a few days start, and it didn't take long to hear back. He telephoned that doors were wide open in Rome and that the believers in the Pentecostal and evangelical churches were very open to sponsoring our meetings.

He mentioned one thing in passing – "I think you guys are going to have to lose the long hair, though. They're not very excited about it down here. And blue jeans and granny gowns aren't their favorite either."

"No problem," we thought, "let's just try to get there. If we can get through the border and into Italy, at least we'll be somewhere instead of this never-never land we've been in for the past few weeks." And so we headed for Italy.

Thanks to Colonel Klink, we were unable to go through Austria, which is the quickest way to get to Italy, so we had to pick our way back through southern Germany to the Swiss border, Konstanz, Germany into Kreuzlingen, Switzerland. Once in

Switzerland, we knew there was only one way to go – south through Zurich, east toward Lichtenstein and then south again and on through the renowned San Bernardino Pass which isn't really a pass, but a tunnel under a pass in the Swiss Alps. It's about 5 miles long and saves unbelievable amounts of time if you're driving.

The problem was that I didn't read Italian or German and as we approached the entry to the tunnel I saw huge signs and flashing warnings that the tunnel was close and that we'd have to stop once inside the tunnel to show our papers. As I processed the warnings through my American filters, memories of Passau returned. Silly me, I thought these warnings meant a customs checkpoint; that we would enter the tunnel in Switzerland and exit in Italy. That was not the case, but by this time I was gun shy and little things were setting me off. What if we showed our papers inside the tunnel and then were turned back? We had the whole nation of Switzerland behind us. We did not have enough money to journey elsewhere – just the hope that we could make it to Rome.

A few miles before the entry to the San Bernardino tunnel there is a failsafe option available to fools like me who choose not to go through the tunnel and under the mountain. It is the intersection of the E43 highway with the town of Splügen. If you like, you can turn left at Splügen and follow SS36, a two-lane highway, over the Alps instead of going through them. Delightful and scenic.

I turned left, impulsively and without thought to
consequences; I turned left, without pulling over to
consult with my caravan comrades bringing up the
rear; I just turned left because I knew that customs
trolls in the tunnel were going to chew us up and
spit us out and going over the mountain was our
only hope. It was insanity run amok. Hadn't we
just tried a shorter, off-the-beaten-path route in
Germany? How did that work out, Joe?

I made the decision without consulting anyone. We
had four trucks to get through the tunnel. The team
had been sent ahead to Italy on our buses and had
no trouble. I suspected it would be different with
the trucks; why, I do not know. So at the last
minute, I turned left - took the left fork in the
highway up the San Bernardino Pass, not through
the San Bernardino Pass. I was driving a semi, and
there were three other medium-size trucks behind
me.

The climb up the mountain was slow, the road grew
narrow very quickly, and we faced many hairpin
turns. I could see the tandem wheels on my trailer
coming precariously close to the edge several times
in some of the turns. Later I would learn that the
team driver behind me just about fainted a couple of
times. The outside wheels of my tandem were
actually hanging over the edge on certain close turns
and knocking rocks and stones over the cliff. He
could see them falling to the bottom hundreds of
feet below us.

It was late October by this time, and we had no clue what the weather on top of the mountain would be like. I began to get a hint at about 9,000 feet because the ground was well covered with snow. By the time we got to the top of the pass at 11,000 feet, the sky clouded over, the snow began to fall, the wind began to blow, and we were in the throes of an alpine blizzard. The two-lane highway quickly became impassable. We slipped and slid on up, but we had no chains (as did all the other drivers) and finally my semi gave one final lurch and began jackknifing and sliding off the road. I couldn't see far enough to know where I might be sliding; there just wasn't time to think about it.

The Swiss drivers were furious with us. Many of them were on their way for a weekend of skiing at St. Moritz, and we blocked the way. Finally the snowplows came and forced the last two trucks in our caravan back down the road to a side park for trucks. By "forced" I mean they nudged up to the front fenders of our trucks with their huge blades and began pushing us back down the mountain.

Our trucks were not new, by any stretch. It was 1974 and the trucks were vintage early '60s. The brakes had locked on one of our trucks and so the wheels screeched and burned all the way down. Another plow hooked its chain onto my front bumper and towed me to the top of the pass. Then he went back and got truck number two. We had very little fuel but were afraid of the engines stalling in the frigid cold over night if we shut them off. So we let them idle all night long. Several girls from the team were with us, since they wouldn't fit in the buses. Fortunately there was a chalet-type hotel at the top of the pass. We had just enough money to put the girls up for the night, and Dave, the other driver, and I stayed in our trucks through the night as the storm howled outside.

The next morning was beautiful – bright sunshine, glistening white snow covering the most incredible mountains I had ever seen. And here we were at the top! The two girls who'd been traveling in the cab of my truck, one of them my future wife, skipped out to the trucks to wake us up. Breakfast came with their rooms; they had become the overnight darlings of the chalet and had spent the night snuggled under down-filled comforters – of course they were skipping! The hills were alive with the sound of music. I was looking at the fuel gauge.

The two smaller trucks made their way up the mountains and went on past us to look for help further down the pass. It wasn't long before Greg came roaring up the mountain in his truck with great news. They'd found a little bungalow along the way owned by a sweet, white-haired widow who spoke textbook English. She was delighted to help us, and so all four trucks were parked along the highway, and we all spent the next night in her beautiful home in the Swiss Alps and ate like kings and queens.

Chapter 23
Passage to Italy

We wound our way down from the San Bernardino Pass in Switzerland, having had enough of the Alps and its snow. At the bottom of the pass, lies the Italian border so the traveler has two options: either make it through this border or turn around and head back up the mountain. Heading back up that mountain was not an option for me, so we resolved to make it through this border and head to Rome.

The Swiss waved us on through, glad to get rid of us, and the Italians – the Italians began by asking if our trucks contained pornographic literature of any kind. It was an amazing moment and I just didn't have an answer. After careful thought, I pointed to the "Christ is the Answer" on the side of the truck, but he didn't seem impressed nor did he seem to understand my explanation. He went into his office, came back out asking for more paperwork and demanded to know the same thing the Austrians wanted to know: "How are you going to live while you're in Italy?" When I told him what we had planned in Rome, he shook his head and said, "You cannot go in. You don't have the proper paper work." (We communicated in French since he refused to speak English, and I knew not one word in Italian; just enough French from high school to get by.)

I was speechless. I hung my head and prayed. "God, I am not going back up that mountain." I followed the guard back into the guard office pleading with him all the way. He refused to change his mind. I sat down on a counter top and again hung my head, this time praying more earnestly in a heavenly language and loud enough so that people in the office could hear me. Perhaps God would give me the gift of tongues in Italian. It didn't matter – I informed God we simply could not go back up those mountains.

The officer disappeared into his cubicle and closed the door. I heard him on the phone speaking loudly with someone. He threw down the receiver with a bang and came back out, marching up to me: "Okay, you can go. Allez! Allez vitement!" We were gone in a heartbeat, and I never figured out if it was the tongues or because I'd made a pest of myself.

The tent location in Rome could not have been better: located on one of the busiest north/south arteries through the city, Via Cristoforo Columbo, and nestled onto a vacant lot surrounded by massive apartment buildings west, south and north and the six-lane avenue to the east. Once we'd arrived, it was easy to forget the difficulties in Austria and Switzerland.

Whereas in mid to northern Europe the public response was mostly muted, Italy was the opposite. From the moment we parked the trucks it was "che cosa," "che fa," "che cosa fa?" (Roughly, "What are you doing here?", not because we were a threat but because they were insatiably curious). Kids from the neighborhood, grandmas and grandpas, moms and babies in strollers – an endless parade of inquisitors, both curious and happy to see our American faces; lots of hand gestures, facial histrionics – I could tell Italy and the American Jesus freaks were going to get along just fine.

One of the first items on our agenda was to get the guys' hair cut and the acquisition of skirts for the ladies in place of their granny gowns. "Hippie" didn't go down well in Italy. It was the first time in three or four years that some of us had cut our hair or shaved our beards – "When in Rome ..."

Chapter 24
Cibo

I want to talk about food now. Seasoned U.S. travelers will know about these things already, and if you're that person, skip to the next chapter. If you haven't traveled to Europe, well ... poor you. I mean it! Get over there!

Backing up a bit, when we arrived in Scandinavia on our first missions trip, we thought we'd died and gone to heaven. People were so generous. We were constantly being invited to peoples' houses for tea and snacks, then more tea, then lunch, then coffee and snacks and on and on. It was amazing compared to lentils and donuts and turnips in America.

My Scandinavian favorites were the hard crackers called knäckebröd (Swedish for "crisp bread") on which we would pile cheese, marmalade, real butter, thin-sliced bologna, anchovies, sardines, or caviar (squeezed out of a toothpaste-type tube.) A typical Swede at snack time would eat maybe one half of a knäckebröd (about the size of half a graham cracker) with assorted condiments. Not us! Tea times and coffee times were treated as if these might be our last meals on earth.

After we began evangelism in earnest, starting in Gothenburg, Sweden, our team of evangelists grew quickly to 125. As the team grew, the invitations to tea declined. And so we were forced to think up ways of feeding ourselves. Potatoes were common. We ate a lot of potato soup. There was some bread and cheese, but it was mostly potatoes.

It was the same in Finland. In Holland we switched from potatoes to macaroni and noodles. It wasn't until we arrived in Italy that we discovered real eating. Italians not only love to eat, they love to share the experience with you. Never have I seen so much food. There were meals when I silently prayed that no more food would be brought to the table. Those few times all occurred in Italy.

"A tavola non si invecchia." (At the table with good friends and family you do not become old.) – Italian folk saying.

Our arrival in Rome produced quite a stir in the evangelical community. Churches and families competed to get us into their homes for meals and fellowship. We were the first group who had come to Rome with a tent and an open style of preaching in the streets.

Sunday afternoons were amazing. After church services in the morning, we were sent to various homes in groups of two and three and the main event would begin. Our evening meal in the U.S., supper, finds its counterpart in the Italian noon feast, or pranza, observed each day. The "mother of main meals" is the Sunday afternoon pranza. I'll never forget my first. Moms and Dads and brothers and sisters and aunts, uncles, cousins, grandmas and grandpas and curious neighbors and friends all gathered in the dining room to welcome us, see us and serve us – a mountain of cibo (chee' boh - Italian for "food") and a chaos of joy. The first course came out – the antipasto (lit. "before the meal"). These were finger foods – olives, crackers, small cuts of bologna, pickles, cheese, etc. I ate too much antipasto, not understanding that in a three or four course meal in Italy you have to pace yourself. I did not do that ... and our hosts were delighted: "Mangia, Mangia!" (mahn'-zhyah) they said, hovering over us; cheerleaders for gluttons. Then came the primo (first course), the most delicious mastaciolli: "Mangia! Mangia!" as I horsed it down, our hosts approaching nirvana. We were going, "Yeah, this is awesome! I could get used to this;" and they were going: "Mangia, mangia!" It was a love fest. Mama could not have been more proud or more flattered.

Fullness is indicated when the hypothalamus, blood sugar levels and stomach and intestines trigger a very simple command to the brain: STOP! Unfortunately there is no such word in Italian relating to gastrointestinal issues nor, it seems, has such a genetic array made it into their body chemistry. So we began to realize that "Italian" meant something more than a language or a culture. It was a predisposition to eat beyond normal human ability. Here is when problems began for us - when the needle in our guts hit "full" and it dawned on us that we were only HALF DONE WITH THE MEAL!

We were stuffed but there is no such thing as "stuffed" in Italy so they were just getting started! Then came secondo: a course of meat, thinly cut steak and salad - and then the formaggio e frutta (cheese and fruit), dolce (sweet desserts) with espresso coffee (a concentrated coffee syrup that could wake the dead). They placed bubbling mineral water, San Pellegrino, on the table at the beginning of the meal for everyone, and we were encouraged to drink along the way. I found out later that it has an important role in the pranza: the gas in the water produces no small amount of belching. This allows the gas build-up in the stomach to escape, which allows more room for more food: the contemporary Italian alternative to the ancient Roman technique of barfing out your meal and returning to the table for more.

I could take no more. My eyes were crossing, and I knew I was about to be seriously sick if I didn't stop. "Mama" kept urging me on. "Mangia, mangia tutti!" she insisted. "Eat! Eat it all!" And so I ate from guilt until I finally held up my hands in surrender. She stood by me, folded her hands over her stomach, glared at me with a half-suppressed smile and shook her head.

After the noon meal, the family conducted us into different bedrooms where we were allowed to take post-feast naps. In Italy this was the siesta. The entire country shut down from one to three in the afternoon (less true today). Stomachs are laid to rest, food is allowed to digest; brains are groggy anyway from the wine, and nothing stirs. No one could buy gas during siesta; you couldn't go to the bank, you couldn't ride the bus, you couldn't buy stamps. Cacophonous, vibrant, jubilant Italy went to sleep after pranza.

It was this way for the ten months we were there – every Sunday afternoon. It quickly made up for the turnips and donuts and, yes, we gained weight.

Wine and Beer

One of our great surprises in Italy was the fact that Christians drank wine – sometimes in large amounts. At first we, being American evangelical teetotalers, declined their offers for the best wine in the house with our meals. We preferred Coke or some other soft drink, thank you. But we began to discover that these people were highly offended that we were refusing their wine. It was definitely a cultural change for us.

Here they were, Pentecostal believers - the women were not allowed to wear makeup or short sleeves. Pants on women were taboo. In church services, the men sat on one side of the church, and the women on the other. All women were required to wear little skullcaps or scarves on their heads as a covering. There was no hugging between members of the opposite sex at church. Men greeted one another with "pace" ("pah'-tchay" or "peace") and a kiss on each cheek. Women did the same. All of this great care in observance of Christian propriety, and then at home, out came the wine.

Eventually we graduated from Coke and Seven-Up to wine, and it really wasn't that bad. Italians never got drunk. They were not like Americans who often drink just to get drunk. And so we followed their lead and had no problems. Wine was like soda pop to them as was beer for our German brothers and sisters. One man's scandal is another man's blessing. Makeup and pants on women here? No problem. Wine on the table there? No problem. We really are different.

One story made its way back to us later on from the first team in Sicily, the small island off the "toe" of the boot in southern Italy. The Sicilians ate a bit differently than those in the north, although there was no diminished quantity. One glorious Sunday afternoon, a few of the team members were invited to the typical Sunday meal and were served in the typical abundant fashion they had come to expect. The meat course was particularly delicious, and they asked their host, after the meal, what kind of meat it was. The interpreter that afternoon said he didn't know the English word for the animal but that it goes, "Hee Haw" when it's excited!

More on food later.

Chapter 25
Three Months in Rome

We had gone from Music City, USA (Nashville) to the City of Music (Vienna) and now to Rome, "The Eternal City." Rome and all of Italy actually exists in a parallel universe, quite apart from anything any Westerner will ever experience. I mean that. No one is ever prepared for Planet Italy; you just adapt; spend enough time there and adaptation turns into delight.

By now I had my own tent since I was leading the group; a small white canvas thing with my own cot and propane heater. As always, the single men slept in one dorm tent (20 feet X 40 feet) and the single women in another just like it. Our business office was now situated in the back end of a large Swedish furniture truck called a möbler which looked like a white, forty-foot version of an American UPS van; Moby Dick with no tail. We also had a 15'X15' kitchen tent and another the same size used for laundry. As in the U.S. our married couples either had their own tents or campers.

Rome had no sewer hook up options, so we dug a large pit behind the tents and emptied wastewater there; but we did manage to acquire city power. We rented porta potties. The tent was an instant object of curiosity to the neighborhood and to passersby. At night, when the music and lights started up, we proved too much for the any resistance the neighborhood could muster and they were drawn in to see for themselves.

I spoke through an interpreter, Luciano Crociani, a wonderful Pentecostal pastor who was respected in the Roman evangelical community. Each night, before the meeting started, Luciano would come to my small tent, bow his six foot four inch frame through the tent entrance and kneel with me to pray for God's favor on the message. We did this every night for three months. Not once did he complain about my living quarters or the lack of heat or the discomfort involved. He was thirty-five years my senior but always showed up.

All of his church was involved – his wife, his son, Gabriel, just a teenager – everyone. I was a frequent guest in their apartment – a harrowing drive through the middle of Rome, around the Coliseum and along the ancient Appian Way. In those days, the stones from the original Appian Way were still in place and were still used as a street; no pavement over them, no sewer grates, no gutters – just massive four foot by four foot stones polished and smooth from over two millennia of use. As we traveled along, you could look out on either side of the car to see the still-existing ruins of viaducts, columns, statues – sitting as they had been left following the demise of the Empire.

Each time, Pastor would pick me up in his light blue VW bug and off we'd go, sometimes to eat, sometimes to speak at his church, sometimes to pray for someone who was sick. My first ride with him was amazing – he ran every red light, just like everyone else. Finally I asked him, "Do Roman drivers feel comfortable about running through these traffic lights?"

His response, "Yes, bruh-thair Joe. You see we believe that those lights are placed there by the government to defy the people. (I did not realize this.) We pay them no mind." This with his right hand held out, fingers straight, hand going around in a circular motion as the shoulders shrugged and the eyebrows raised as if to say, "What are you gonna do?"

Street witnessing in Rome was surreal. The Eternal City was not just home to Italians, but to every culture and language in the world. We camped out at the main train station most days, an enormous, Quonset-hut-type structure that never had a quiet moment. We also chose to test the waters on the campus of the University of Rome where 80,000 students were enrolled, again from every corner of the globe.

The student union on campus was definitely the center of all social activity and had become, unbeknownst to us, the "territory" of the student Communist party. They had been there for years, occupying the space on the marble patio leading into the building, and woe to the person or group who felt it was their right to coexist in that space. We did just that – and were warned on the first day that we could not be there. We objected and insisted that it was public property (it was) and they insisted right back that we go find somewhere else to talk about Jesus because He didn't have their permission in that spot.

About two or three days later, it was obvious we had stepped on the dragon's tail, and he was furious. The student-led Communists had certain male muscle guys who became our daily cross, bursting out of the crowd whenever they would see us, warning, cursing and manhandling us if necessary. Well, it was always necessary because we weren't leaving. No police ever showed up. The thugs molested our girls, stole our literature and Bibles and often burned them in plain sight on the steps of the student union. We were escorted (bum-rushed actually) onto the street running in front of the union, sometimes pushed out, sometimes dragged out, sometimes slugged. But we always came back and the non-Communist students always tried defending us, but there was no back down from the Commies, either, so we endured their persecution daily for three months.

Later we learned that many of them were part of the Red Brigades, an Italian terrorist group. They eventually discovered that we called ourselves "Christ is the Answer" which lent itself to an obvious American conspiracy: Christ is the Answer, CITA which, when properly deciphered, was code for C-I-A. Word quickly spread among them that we were CIA and from then on we were often jeered and mocked: "Ci – A, Ci – A!" (Chee – yah, Chee – yah!), because, of course, it would be standard CIA procedure to operate out in the open on the campus of a university under cover of the gospel of Jesus Christ with the clear political agenda of introducing people to Christ. We were so busted.

Mohammed was from Somalia, a student at the university and very curious about what we were doing there. He'd seen the conflict between the Communists and us; he'd watched us getting thrown into the street day after day. He wanted to know more and approached me – "Who are you guys? (He spoke English and Italian) Why do you keep coming back after they treat you like that?" I shared, he listened and Mohammed decided he wanted to hear more. That night he found his way to the tent meeting and had more questions after the meeting.

We became good friends and he seemed to love listening to me open up the scriptures even though he'd been raised a Muslim. After several meetings, he wondered openly if it might be better for me to speak through an interpreter at the Student Union on campus, and couldn't I communicate with more people that way? I agreed and said, "What about you? Why don't you think about being my interpreter? I'll get on the steps leading up to the Union building, you can stand beside me and we'll make a go of it."

He smiled and sort of laughed to himself, a gentle, tall, thin, bespectacled man with light African skin and a goatee, and cleared his throat, "Well, I suppose I could try."

"Good, I'll meet you there to tomorrow around one o'clock and let's see what happens."

And I showed up at one, but he was late; about an hour late, and I was beginning to think that the sermon with an interpreter thing wasn't going to happen. And then, there he was, out in the crowd but hardly charging his way up to the front. I actually had to go into the crowd to get him, grabbed him by the arm and we made our way to the Union steps. I could tell he was scared to death – head down, totally out of his element. Mohammed was taking the biggest step of his life – a Muslim, about to speak of the saving grace of Jesus Christ to a crowd of rowdy Communists.

I spoke up: "Attenzione! Attenzione!" And then launched into my public message about how Christ had changed my life. I completed two sentences. Mohammed spoke so softly as my interpreter that I could barely hear him, and we were standing side by side. And then the thugs broke through the crowd, grabbed me under both of my arms, hustled me out the gate and threw me in the street. I remember hearing him say to me as I was being carried off: "I'm sorry." I never saw him again.

We visited the Vatican often, as tourists, then later as tourist guides to family and friends. We tried speaking with people in Vatican Square but were rebuffed by the palace guards each time. One of our group tried reasoning with a guard one day: "Sir, we're just Christians trying to share about Jesus. Why won't you allow this here in Christianity's center?"

"Ma'am," he said, "if Saint Peter himself came here to preach, we would not allow it."

So much for ecumenism.

I asked Gayle to marry me on Christmas Eve, 1974 in Rome. She said, "Yes." Thank you, Gayle. I love you!

Earlier in December the Circus Orfei came to town. Circus Orfei was, at that time, one of the largest and most famous of the traveling circuses in Europe. It also happened that they selected a tent site only two blocks north of us on Via Cristoforo Colombo. Tent people stick together. We heard they had arrived and some of our guys went to help them put up their tent, and we became good friends with the whole traveling troupe.

One of the clowns, a tall, blond fellow from England named Steve, became a very close friend. There were also three African American brothers from Brooklyn who had an incredible unicycle act which included unicycle basketball a la Harlem

Globetrotters. Each night, after our meetings were over and our tent shut down, we would walk over to the Circus and watch and hang out with the performers at the completion of their final performance. Steve and the unicycle brothers soon started visiting our tent and talking with us about their spiritual journeys. On New Year's Eve, our band, the Joyful Noise, was invited to play for the Circus performers' New Year's Eve party at their tent. What a blast; from Swedish iron ore mines, to Russian battleships, to Viennese discos to the Circus Orfei – what a long and winding road; pure joy and wonder.

Chapter 26
The Trip to India

Gayle and I were married on March 15, 1975 in the U.S. We continued traveling with the tent team in the U.S. for the next three years. Times were changing; there was much less interest in our street witness and smaller attendance in the meetings. It was as if someone had simply turned off a spigot. We were doing nothing different from what we had done three years previous, but very little response.

It's perplexing when this happens in ministry because you don't see it coming. One day you're successful and productive and the next, it seems, people have lost interest, the audience dwindles and you're left with an empty feeling of having failed somewhere. I've seen it happen to good people in ministry in many places, and still have no explanation. Ok, if the evangelist is cruising for prossies at night after the close of the meeting, I get that; I can see why God might shut that spigot.

About the same time as response was declining in our American outreach, response was picking up in other parts of the world. We connected with a respected South Indian pastor, Sam Chelladurai, from Madras (now called Chennai). Sam challenged us: "How can you justify your continued preaching that Jesus is coming again to people in America, when millions of my people have never heard He came the first time?"

His question cut us and challenged us. We immediately began planning to send our next tent team to India; only Sam helped us understand – "You won't need to bring a tent to India" – and we soon found out why.

Bill, our fearless leader, and Doug, one of our team leaders in Europe, went to India to join Pastor Sam in several crusades he had planned prior to their arrival. I remember Bill and Doug both saying that on their first night in India they decided to get on the next plane and fly back to Europe. The culture, the food, the heat, the discomfort, the bugs, the smell, the dirt and millions of people ... everywhere people ... were so overwhelming they didn't see how they could continue. It was a two-man panic attack. Enter Pastor Sam – I'm not sure what transpired the next morning, but he persuaded them to stay and they stayed.

Their first experience was mind-boggling – tens of thousands of people crowding onto a large parade ground normally used for cricket and soccer. When they returned to the U.S. it was obvious that something very important had transpired, and Christ is the Answer began making plans to send its first team to India.

The first group left for India in 1976 from Europe traveling over 9,000 miles overland through some very dangerous places in Turkey, Iran, Afghanistan and Pakistan. They had purchased a used Mercedes bus and Mercedes van which carried them through deserts, blizzards, mountain passes and stretches of road known for highway robbers all the way to the southern tip of India, Palayamkottai, a small suburb of the city of Tirunelveli, just 50 miles from the Indian Ocean.

One event stands out from memories of their reports in letters and communication later on. Doug told me about the snowstorm in eastern Turkey. It was October when they traveled, and the roads in eastern Turkey were treacherous enough without the snow. But a snowstorm happened, and they were caught in it. Highways in those mountains have a tendency to disappear, and one is left with the option of picking one's way through the desert until the road reappears. You could follow a truck driver, but it was difficult to keep up with them. And they were crazy, and they wanted to get their trips over with. Turks are mostly Muslim and Turkish truck drivers do believe! As a matter of fact, on the front of many of their trucks are written one of two phrases: "Inshallah" or Bismallah." The first means, "If God Wills," and the second, "In the name of God." We interpreted the first to mean, "If God wills it, I will arrive at my destination, but I'm not so sure about you." So what that philosophy did was give room for them to drive like banshees, and if they happened to take themselves out and you out in the process, it was all the will of God! I'm not sure what the other meant – maybe, "In the name of God, get out of the way!"

The snowstorm caught them by surprise. They had no snow tires and no chains and were on mountain roads. Inevitably, the bus came upon a hill and curve it simply could not negotiate. It began to slide backward and off the side of the road, partially blocking the highway. The truck drivers did have chains and were not inclined to share. They just wanted them out of the way. After they began to collect in a line behind our guys' vehicles on the highway waiting for the bus to be moved, they could take it no more. This was not God's will.

When they first approached the bus, Doug thought they wanted to help. That was not the case. They collectively got behind the bus and began shoving it to the side of the highway, and kept shoving ... and shoving. Doug quickly determined that their intention was to just push the whole bus over the side of the cliff with the team in it; not rational but convenient. Somehow, some way, a Hand stopped them from committing the whole team to instant martyrdom, and they backed off and drove on. And somehow the team was able to get over the mountains of eastern Turkey and go on to India – inshallah.

The reports back were welcome news, our first missionaries to Asia had arrived safe and bedraggled and were now housed and getting ready for their first outreach activities. It's hard to explain the kind of courage they had shown making this first pioneering sort of trip the way they did with very little money and no assurance of a good outcome.

To this day I feel dwarfed by their faith and moxie but still have to confess I'm glad I was not on that first trip. It was a year and a half before Gayle and I were approached about the possibility of being on the second team. We knew it was our turn to take the plunge.

Chapter 27
Riders on the Storm

Riders on the storm
Riders on the storm
Into this house we're born
Into this world we're thrown
Riders on the storm. - Jim Morrison

In the late sixties and early seventies, it was fashionable for counter-culture folks like us, to visit Amsterdam, Holland and partake of the wild cornucopia of drugs and sex available with no legal restrictions. Heroine, hashish and marijuana were sold openly in the central plaza downtown along with all the paraphernalia needed to inhale it or shoot it up. Amsterdam quickly became for world-wise hippies of all cultures what the Haight-Ashbury could only have aspired to in San Francisco. Amsterdam was Haight-Ashbury on steroids, literally and figuratively. It was nothing to go to the post office to mail a letter and see a waif-like 15-year-old on the steps outside shooting up heroine or breathing in toxic fumes from a paper bag full of plastic cement. You could purchase needles and syringes right there at the post office.

There were numerous ragtag travel agencies in Amsterdam that catered to the hippies. The agencies owned or had access to a fleet of small, run-down buses and vans complete with experienced drivers and tour guides. And they had one destination – India. Kids were flocking to

India. News traveled fast – hippies could go there – the ones who practiced transcendental meditation - and find a guru and an ashram (a commune for disciples of a guru) and local hashish or marijuana or whatever suited one's fancy. When they became bored with the guru, there was always Goa. Goa is the Indian version of Newport Beach, California. Located on the west coast of India, the beaches are beautiful, the weather is unbelievable, and the local people, mostly Roman Catholic, were not as opposed to western visitors as were Indians in other parts of the country. And so this became the end of the hippie trail.

The hippie trail wound through western Europe, then eastern Europe (Yugoslavia and Greece), Turkey, Iran, Afghanistan, Pakistan and India. Once completed, travelers had gone close to 10,000 miles through some of the most remote and forbidding places on the planet. We'd received news from various sources in Amsterdam about what to expect, but expecting and experiencing turned out to be very different.

Our turn came in October of 1978. By that time, we had our first child, Amie, who had just turned two years old. We flew to Europe from the States and drove to Italy to join the Christ is the Answer traveling team in Catania, Sicily. Three Mercedes diesel vans had been purchased for us in Munich, Germany, and we stayed in Catania just long enough for the mechanics to outfit them for the journey ahead.

We had supplies but not the kind you might think. The first teams to India had learned from experience what to take and what not to take on the hippie trail. For example we took lots of used U.S. blue jeans and baseball caps and American-made t-shirts; and perfume and ladies' soaps were good, too. These were all meant as gifts to people - well, actually, officials - whom we would meet along the way. We found that border guards in Afghanistan and Pakistan enjoyed taking home American-made perfume to their wives. And gas station attendants in Iran were more than happy to barter their diesel fuel for our blue jeans. And that's how it happened.

Just as we left Catania, I picked up a fellow traveler – a going-away present from Italy - who decided to make the trip to India with me. His first name was Amoebic and his surname Dysentery. I became his host and tour guide for the trip. I would not wish amoebic dysentery on my worst enemy. I had it the entire trip. The main symptom of dysentery is unending, miserable diarrhea. The first few days of sickness are the worst – I didn't know where I was because I wasn't conscious. All I remember is crawling into a bathroom somewhere in Italy in a house where we stayed until I could get well enough to travel. After two days we were able to go, but the diarrhea stayed with me the whole trip. I think the amoeba had a long-lost cousin in India.

We drove twenty-four hours a day for twenty-one days and put over 9,000 miles behind us. These were not interstate highway miles. The most breathtaking view was coming down off of a bluff overlooking Istanbul and seeing the Straits of Bosporus stretched out in front of us. It was magnificent.

Istanbul is an amazing city. It is ancient Constantinople, named after Emperor Constantine, who made Christianity the national religion in the Roman Empire. There are almost no traces of Christianity in Turkey even though many of the earliest Gentile churches were birthed through the preaching of the apostle Paul in its cities. The gigantic Blue Mosque in downtown Istanbul had once been an orthodox cathedral, we were told. Now it stood only as a Muslim shrine.

Since we hadn't bathed in a few days, it was time to use the Turkish baths. These were huge steam rooms, fed by natural springs and steam, we were told, and it was great to sit and let the steam burn off the traveling grunge that had collected on our bodies. This was part of the hippie trail routine, we learned, and we saw many hippies in the neighborhood of the baths. We slept in the vans that night just across the street from the Blue Mosque and took off for points east the next morning.

Do You Know the Way to Dogubayazit?

The hardest part of the trip was still ahead of us. We stopped for an afternoon in Ankara, Turkey's capitol, visited with a local missionary there who was teaching at the local university and went on. Eastern Turkey is unbelievable. Its roads are always two lanes, sometimes one. If they are paved, then there are endless potholes. But when you get into the mountains, the pavement often disappears, and gravel is what's left; and where there's gravel, there is dust - lots of dust - dust that reminds you of something out of Lawrence of Arabia. We choked and sputtered our way through the mountains for hundred of miles. No one could get clean. The bumping and jarring seemed endless. It was miserable.

There was no travel at night in eastern Turkey. Twice the Turkish army stopped us as the sun went down and forced us to camp out all night on the side of the road. Night bandits were common on those long stretches of desolate road, and they took no prisoners. We had heard stories of cars and buses being stopped, everyone being shot and all their belongings looted. So Turkish soldiers camped around us on those nights, and I really didn't mind it.

Of course one of the most famous mountains in the world, Ararat, is in eastern Turkey. It was mid-morning when we pulled off the highway to just sit, look at it in the distance and take pictures. But I have to back up to explain what happened next. Before we entered Turkey we were warned not to hand out Christian literature along the way. It was considered illegal propaganda by the Turkish government, Turkey being a Muslim country.

We had not realized that one of our well-meaning brothers had been passing out literature anyway whenever we'd make a stop at a gas station or restaurant. The wrong people got hold of some of those pamphlets, and the police finally caught up with us as we were snapping pictures of the great mountain where Noah's ark came to rest. Two police vans pulled up in back of our vehicles and a police cruiser blocked us in front. The arresting officer came up to my van, the lead van, and told me to open the door. He climbed inside and sat down in the front passenger seat. The other officers did the same in the other two vans. He motioned me to go back. I tried asking why and what for in English, but it was futile. He just got more angry and threatening. I looked back at Doug, and he motioned to just cooperate. I was scared stiff.

We went into the town nearby, Dogubayazit, through dusty streets and straight into the police compound. All three of our vehicles were brought in, and the high, steel gates closed behind us and were locked. I knew we were in big trouble. The compound was an interesting place. Huge marijuana plants grew in a specially terraced garden within the walls. The officers guarding us would stroll over to the plants once in awhile, pick some ripe berries off the stems and eat them. It added to the moment, really, knowing that our guards, with loaded weapons, were stoned out of their minds.

One consolation was that they fell instantly in love with Amy, our two-year-old daughter. It was as if they had never seen a sight like her. She was cute, blond-headed and pink-skinned. And she was really taken with their prayer beads. One guard knelt down and let her play with them. It really took the edge off for the moment.

The police captain came up to Doug and me and immediately started asking us what we had in the vans. He was a frightening man – kind of a balding version of Lee Marvin with a hair-trigger temper. He wanted Doug to take him and show him the vans. Doug didn't move fast enough, and he grabbed Doug by the shirtsleeve, threw him to the ground ripping the sleeve completely off and yelled, "Go!" We got the picture.

They emptied the vans, found the literature and confiscated all of it. They led us into the police station and told us to wait. The captain came out after making a few calls and informed us we would be going back to another town 200 hundred kilometers in the direction from which we had just come to face a judge there. We were charged with illegal distribution of Christian propaganda.

We were told to climb back into the vans, now with a full police escort, and to head back west to face the judge. We left the compound all wondering what God was going to do for us now, but then it became apparent He had other plans. Two things happened which, in hind sight, seem to have been God things.

First we needed fuel in our vans to make the long trip back, and there was only one gas station on the outskirts of town. We pulled in with police in tow. No diesel. The gas station had no diesel. They wouldn't be getting their next shipment of diesel until the next day. (We ran into that frequently in eastern Turkey.) So we headed back to the compound, and the captain stewed.

Next came the second intervention - Doug asked if we could go next door to the telephone office so we could call the U.S. embassy in Ankara and, surprisingly, the captain let us out. The rest of the group had to stay put, but Doug's next move proved to be our salvation. He went across the street to change some money for more Turkish lira while I waited in the telephone office to contact the embassy. While he was in the bank, he met a Turkish army captain who spoke perfect English. He asked what was going on because he'd heard about the stir with our vehicles being impounded. Doug explained what had happened, that we didn't mean to break the law, and could this man do something?

He did indeed. He went with Doug to see the captain. Every officer including the police captain snapped to attention as he entered the room and a cup of Turkish tea was in his hand in an instant. There was animated discussion between him and the captain in the next room as the army officer negotiated our release in such a way that the captain would not lose face. He came out, told Doug to follow him down to the local courthouse, (there was a judge here after all!) and Doug and a couple of the drivers appeared before the judge. He slapped our wrists, confiscated Bibles and literature and told us to get out of the country. No problem. The Iranian border was 70 kilometers down the road. Imagine that – being relieved to enter Iran! That night we slept in our vans on the Iran border outpost and knew we'd just had a very close call. Other believers had been caught in the same way in Turkey and had spent weeks and even months in prison.

The Journey through Iran

October 1978 was not a good time to be in Iran. We woke up at the border station the next morning to hear from the border guards that there had been riots in the streets the night before. Islamic fundamentalist students had been demonstrating against the Shah and many had been killed. These were the pre-natal weeks leading to the Iranian revolution and the removal of the Shah from power in favor of Ayatollah Khomeini. The students' funerals were held that morning, and you could cut the air with a knife. Hundreds gathered in the cemetery not far from the highway. The soldiers told us not to linger in town. Anti-American sentiment was high. We quickly fueled up and headed east toward Tehran.

Doug was right. American blue jeans were great items to have along. We used them at every fuel

station along the way. Diesel fuel for blue jeans –
who knew?

We didn't spend long in Tehran. There was too
much unrest. We continued east to the holy city of
Mashhad where Doug knew of an officer in the army
who had taken us in before. We found him; he took
us to the bathhouse and then treated us all to a
wonderful dinner. We wasted no time in Iran. The
next day we were off to Afghanistan.
The Afghan Border

It was no problem leaving Iran. It was something
else entering Afghanistan. We knew right away it
would be different. The ancient trade routes came
through here. As far as these people were
concerned, the old trade routes were fine the way
they were. This western border looked more like a
Wild West frontier outpost. Signs directing us to
where to park were perched on crooked stakes along
side the road, hand-painted in Farsi or Urdu, black
on white and faded after years of neglect. I kept
looking for an arrow banner pointing toward
Tombstone. There was nothing in English. So we
picked our way along to an enormous area in the
desert, unpaved, cluttered with a hundred or more
vehicles – diesel buses with luggage racks running
the entire length of the vehicle stacked with bundles
five feet high full of peoples' belongings, bedding,
clothing – each bundle the sum total of a family's
earthly possessions -five gallon plastic containers
full of kerosene, baskets full of live animals,
chickens probably, and the inside of the buses

jammed with human beings – and more chickens. Along with the buses were an assortment of diesel trucks of all sizes and a few automobiles that could have been taxis or hired cars, also piled high with bundles and pieces of luggage.

There were two one-story shacks – mud brick with corrugated tin roofs – side by side, which served as offices for the border guards. We would soon find out why Doug had us bring along things like perfume and American-made baseball caps. The border guards were busy elsewhere for the moment. It was easy to tell which bus drivers had figured out the border crossing routine and which ones hadn't. Bus drivers with adequate savvy had paid their bribes, the guards had done a quick, token search through the vehicles, the people had been let back on board and were on their way. Those drivers who had refused to bribe the guards were now paying for their neglect. Not only were their people told to get off the bus, the entire load on top was being taken apart piece by piece. Some of these buses, we found out, would be at this border for two or more days waiting for these guards to finish their inspection.

Doug disappeared into the guardhouse with a pair of blue jeans and some perfume. Sam Hobson, one of our drivers who'd made this trip before, went with him. Within 30 minutes they re-emerged with one of the "guards." He was about eighteen years old and looked more like a shepherd than an officer. He was wearing Sam's blue jean jacket under his officer jacket and Sam's bright yellow baseball cap with the Caterpillar logo. I could see Sam was not amused. The kid tried hard to act official, but it was a joke. "My name is Charlie Chaplin, and I'll be your guard today!" It took Charlie about a half-hour to "search" us. Every minute or so he'd look at something in one of our trucks, point at it, ask Doug in Pashtu what it was, Doug would tell him in English, he would nod as if he understood, his brow knit together in a very official-looking knit, and he'd go on to the next vehicle. This little dance complete, he got out, shook Doug's hand, smiled and waved him back into his offices where our passports were stamped – well, – smudged, and we were sent on our way. The last we saw of Charlie, he was headed for the next bus in his yellow baseball cap yelling to the driver to take everything off the roof. No baseball cap, no break.

What a Country!

America and Russia built the only major highway in Afghanistan. We built the first half. Actually we paid for the first half. On a map it looks like a huge "U" with one end starting its dip at Herat, straight south to Kandahar and the upside of the dip ending at Kabul the capital. The highway was about the only twentieth century item we saw during our journey down and up the "U." Gas stations were sparse. Towns and villages resembled something out of the first installment of Star Wars. And we met our first nomads.

They were camped about 400 yards off the highway shortly after we entered the country. From a distance their tents looked like low, black hills elevated slightly from the barren, light brown landscape. We pulled over, got out our cameras and proceeded cautiously. Halfway to the huddle of tents a twelve-year-old boy who was tending the goats and sheep along with a small brother and a couple of dogs, approached with a curious look – not welcoming, not smiling – but obviously curious; cautious but friendly. He allowed us to take his picture with the tents in the background. We gestured toward the tents and held up our cameras. His reply was instant – a shake of the head sideways and a wagging finger helped us understand this was as far as we could go.

We motioned a "thank-you" and turned toward the highway, but he motioned back that he wanted us to wait a minute. He ran off to the tents and came back in a minute with a small package wrapped in old newspaper. I opened it and found a stack of flat bread, fresh-baked under a cow-dung fire inside the tents. Villagers and nomads in much of Asia gather cow dung from their farm animals, form the dung into eight-inch-wide patties, set them out in the sun to dry and use them for cooking fuel. If you've ever eaten anything cooked over a cow-dung fire, you'll remember the distinct flavor. When you cook burgers over charcoal, it leaves a charcoal flavor. When you bake bread over dried cow dung patties ... we thanked him for the bread (we had to taste it in front of him as a courtesy), and took off for points east.

We stayed with friends in the capital of Kabul for a night. We woke up to festivities throughout the city. It was Flag Day, and everyone was hanging their red, Communist party flags from balconies and out windows. The government was forcing people to display their flags – anything to placate the Russians to the north who had helped install the present government in Kabul. Within a year, the Soviet armies would invade Afghanistan.

Camels and Why We Hate Them

After navigating the famous Khyber Pass to the east of Kabul through the Hindu Cush Mountains, we arrived at the border of Pakistan. Again it was a scene out of ancient history. The road and the border checkpoint were cut into a hillside and 500 feet below, in a large, open valley, were the camel trains. Yes, camel trains, just like the ones that carried spices to the west from China centuries ago. The camels and their herders continue to use these ancient routes carrying goods to and fro, although I'm not sure what they carry or to where they carry it.

Doug had told me about how interesting this border was and how fun it was to take camel rides while waiting to be checked through customs. He had the kind of look on his face, though, that said, "I know something you don't."

We proceeded down the steep path to the valley with cameras in hand. I volunteered to be the first "rider." Doug, knowing the terrain and the customs, marched over to a group of three herders and began negotiating a ride for me on one of their camels. No problem. He signaled me over to the group, and they led me over to one of their beasts that happened to be sitting at the moment enjoying a quiet rest in the 100-degree afternoon heat.

The herder motioned for me to climb on board in back of the hump. Of course, when I did, the camel lumbered to its feet, and I found myself much higher in the air than I wanted to be. It was a huge camel.

I was not at all ready for what happened next. You see, what I did not know was that this particular camel did not belong to any of these three men. His owner was off having tea, and they were just keeping their eye on him. He wouldn't move, as a result, so they thought of a clever idea to get him moving. Picking up small stones, they started to pelt the camel. It worked. He not only moved, he began to BUCK, like a crazed rodeo bronco. I could only grab onto the hair on the hump and hold on for dear life. There is a certain wild-west tradition one expects when watching a cowboy riding a rodeo horse. The horse is graceful as he leaps and twists. The cowboy, if he knows what he's doing, flops around on the horse's back for a few seconds until the horse realizes he's whipped and then gives up. But I had never seen a camel jump and buck, and this was not the rodeo. This was an absolute cartoon – no graceful leaps or twists, just a huge, awkward, gangly, stupid beast shaking and snarling and jerking in three different directions at once trying to rid itself of this pest on its back.

During one brief moment between bucks, I looked back and noticed Doug filming me with his 8mm movie camera, beside himself with laughter, and the herders having a gay old time throwing stones and laughing along with Doug. My wife and daughter were looking on in horror. Well, I wasn't smart enough at this point to jump off. The camel was in a free-for-all panic, and I wasn't about to take a leap and risk being trampled under his huge hooves. Since he couldn't get me off his back, Mr. Pachyderm decided another tactic might work. He stopped jumping and craned his long neck backward toward me and began biting at my feet and legs. I pushed myself back just in time to avoid his teeth and serious injury. I learned later from people on a wildlife farm in California that they had seen a camel crane its neck over a low fence, grab a Shetland pony grazing near the fence, pull him over the fence and trample him to death. I can only imagine what he could have done to me.

Well, he couldn't buck me, and he couldn't bite me, so there was only one thing left to do. He turned his head toward me, craned back as close as he could get and simply bellowed as loud and as angrily as possible. Now camels chew obscene amounts of cud, which is nothing more than regurgitated straw and grass, and this camel had a mouthful. I was literally sprayed from head to foot with this rancid, manure-like substance. That was the final straw, literally. I decided, "Hey, I'm gonna die if I stay up here, so why not make a run for it?" I pushed off the back of the camel, as he continued trying to buck, and headed in the opposite direction as fast as I could. Everyone except my wife and daughter was still laughing wildly, and the camera was still rolling. It was days before I could get rid of the smell. I still hate camels. And it will take a miracle of inner healing before I can forgive that camel. There are beasts of burden, and then there are crazy ass beasts of burden, the camel belonging to the latter. It was then I began to understand why they are called camel herders and not camel riders.

Somewhere in Doug's archives lays the 8mm film of that incident. I'm convinced he's kept it all these years for the sole purpose of blackmail. Never let anyone talk you into a camel ride. Ever.

Our Arrival in India

We'd traveled almost 8,000 miles as we crossed the border into our destination country, India. There were still four or more days to go to reach our final destiny near Mumbai (formerly Bombay). After having blessed the Pakistani and Indian border guards with perfume for their wives, we were off.

We traveled at night, which is not a wise thing to do in India just as it had not been in Turkey. Our first night on the highway, we were stopped at a checkpoint by police. They asked if we intended on continuing to the next checkpoint that night, and we said, "Yes." Then they insisted on sending an armed guard with us.

Northern Indian highways are infested with robbers called dacoits. As in Turkey, these people rob buses, trucks, automobiles and whatever else comes down the road. They kill the passengers, take their belongings and disappear into the jungle. That is why we had an armed guard - of sorts. He carried a 75-year-old Enfield, sliding bolt carbine rifle – shoot once, cock the rifle, shoot again. His presence was more like a padlock on a bank vault – more of an insult to would-be robbers than anything else. As I've said, angels were watching over us, and we were keeping them busy.

We pulled into Amritsar, the holy city of the Sikh religion, shortly after visiting the breathtaking Taj Mahal in the city of Agra earlier. There is a huge, gilded temple (Harmandir Sahib or Golden Temple) set in the middle of a 500-yard-wide lake that is enclosed in a walled portion of the downtown district. We left our shoes at the outside doors, as everyone had to, and went in. There were thousands of people inside this compound milling about in a very hushed manner. Vendors sold incense and indulgences around the outer edges of the lake. There were four low-slung, aqueduct-type structures placed like four spokes in a wheel, bridges over the lake, which led out to the golden shrine. Each spoke seemed to move as unbroken lines of people went into and away from the solid gold temple sitting in the middle of the lake. They all moved slowly, with dignity and reverence.

We followed the line across one of the spokes and were awestruck with the design and extravagance of the inside of the temple. It was filled with holy men, some offering prayers, some burning incense at golden altars, some playing and singing and chanting. The incense was so thick we could hardly breathe.

Amy was bedazzled. Her two-year-old eyes had never taken in something like this; Aladdin's cave, the stuff of a Robert Louis Stevenson novel; the incarnation of the Arabian Nights. We ascended the steps to the second floor balcony where we could look down over a brass railing on a group of musicians and singers on the first floor in the center of the shrine offering up songs, a 24/7 stream of Sikh praise and worship. As we moved along the balcony, there was a gasp from someone in the crowd and worried mumbling. There in the middle of the floor, in one of the holiest places in India, was a little puddle. Amie, barely two-years-old and doing her best to hold it in, couldn't anymore and had left her mark. One felt a riot coming on. Doug, having been here before and knowing the possible consequences of this desecration, whispered hoarsely, "Just keep moving – do not go back, do not try to clean it up." And we continued on, quickly and quietly, out of the Golden Temple and on to the final destination.

Poona

It took another two or three days to reach Poona. The original team members who had come on the first journey were already there preparing for our big crusade. Poona lies a hundred miles or so east of Bombay perched on the rim of the Deccan Plateau. It's a very large, very prosperous city, and we were situated in a church compound that had been built around the turn of the twentieth century.

It was an unbelievable relief to get there. I've never felt more exhausted. As we settled into our living quarters, we were informed that, the previous night, on the porch right outside our room, one of the men on the team had run into a king cobra about eight feet long. Welcome to India.

One of the guys in the team came up to me with a greeting and a hug as we stepped out of the van. "Hi, brother, my name is Mitch. Who are you?" I wouldn't have minded except that he knew me, and we had worked together for years. What I hadn't realized was that my little traveling partner, Mr. Dysentery, the one I'd picked up in Sicily and who continued to affect me throughout the trip to India, had caused severe weight loss. I was so thin, my friend, Mitch, didn't recognize me. The journey had taken its toll.

Chapter 28
Telling Others

As far as I can tell, from reading the gospels, Jesus seldom preached in conventional places. He traveled with his twelve, and they would stop at the most unusual spots – water wells, sheep pastures, graveyards, living rooms, hillsides, boats, hog farms, funerals – and in these places, Jesus would feel a sermon coming on. And the most extraordinary things would happen – people would respond right on the spot. They would "believe on Him" the gospels tell us; and blind eyes would open and demons would come out of people and those who were dead would rise to life. In an age where we put a major premium on creating a "spiritual" atmosphere in the sanctuary so the preacher can work his magic, Jesus' methods don't add up. Because we kept finding ourselves in those early years in unusual spots, it didn't seem strange to us to find ourselves preaching in places not normally connected with church. To our surprise and wonder, God would show up.

We were prepared for the unusual at first by using downtown American street corners for our pulpits. In the early seventies, before sophisticated American sinners got wise to the street-corner Jesus freaks popping up all over, a street corner was a great place to witness. Along with the drunks and prostitutes and drug addicts, we would also run into business people, shoppers and commuters who didn't mind stopping for a few minutes to talk with us about the Bible. For a while the streets of America were wonderful places to speak with unbelievers about the God they didn't believe in.

I prayed with all kinds of people: runaways running, businessmen on lunch break, housewives shopping, students getting off school. We ran into Native Americans, priests, lawyers, country western stars, massage therapists doubling as prostitutes (one was a Sunday School teacher at the largest Baptist church in Nashville), transvestites, mob hit men, people running from mob hit men, police, truck drivers, teachers, atheists, agnostics, Bill Cosby, Marty Robbins, Mick Jagger, Jesus (well, he thought he was Jesus), Napoleon (ditto), and a cast of thousands of others.

Most of them walked on by. Sometimes they stopped to talk. Sometimes they grew angry, swore at us and threatened to punch us out. Sometimes they didn't just threaten to punch us out, and someone would get hurt. We were spit on, cursed, mocked, molested, robbed, jeered, and despised. Being ignored was, by far, the most painful because we knew they weren't just ignoring us.

Jesus Had Hillsides, We Had a Tent

I first preached in a tent. I was leading worship but had never preached. One night, while I was in the middle of a song, someone passed a note up to me. Bill, our leader, had become ill and couldn't make it up. The note was to let me know I was the preacher that night. The tent was packed, and I had not one note prepared for a sermon. There had been no time to study or even think about what I might want to say.

The Lord promised His disciples that when they appeared before magistrates and kings, they were not to fear – that He would, by the Spirit, put things in their mouths to say. I opened my Bible that night and found the same thing to be true. There was plenty to say. It's just that what I now know as the Holy Spirit had to kind of take over. I became the vessel and the mouthpiece, and He provided the message. I've never fully understood how that transpires; I can't describe it.

Sometimes the tent was full and at other times the tent was almost empty. As the years went by, we procured larger and larger tents, but we found having a large tent never insures having a large crowd. I remember our meetings in Anaheim, California. We set the tent up on some of the most expensive real estate in southern California, two blocks from Disneyland and across the street from Anaheim Stadium, home of baseball's Los Angeles Angels. By then we had a three-hundred-foot-long tent – yes, the same length as a football field – and we decided to put it all up (you could set tents up in sections instead of having to put up the whole thing.) We anticipated large California crowds and got the opposite. Attendance averaged about five to ten people a night. I became accustomed to preaching to our team members and the faithful "ten." And it's in meetings like that when you discover if God has called you to preach, or if you shouldn't perhaps be out selling insurance.

Preaching in tents is unusual because you're more open to the elements and other sundry distractions. Thunderstorms could be terrifying for our poor guests. As the winds would pick up, the tent would begin to flap violently, the large half-poles would lift off the ground with the flapping. We were often reduced to hanging on to the poles in some puny effort to try to hold things together. Several times over the years, we had to run for it as the wind would catch the tent just right, lift it off its moorings and shred it like forlorn tissue in a matter of seconds. It's a miracle no one was ever injured.

Winter weather was a challenge. We often held meetings in cold, snowy weather even though we migrated south in November. At first we had small kerosene space heaters that barely took the chill off. Later, after visiting a couple of circuses in Italy, we discovered something much better, the mother of all space heaters. A twenty-foot trailer was welded together. Next a six-foot-high squirrel cage fan, like those used on commercial-size air conditioners, was welded onto the frame of the trailer with the blast of the fan pointing toward the front of the trailer. The fan would turn with the help of a six horse, 220-volt electric motor. After that a huge oval tube was welded from one-sixteenth inch thick sheet metal. The tube was fifteen feet long and six feet high. It, in turn, was welded onto the trailer frame in front of the squirrel cage fan. Suspended from inside of the top of the large tube were four burners. These burners, each five inches in diameter and a foot in length, were made from the cylinder sleeves of large diesel truck engines. There was pressurized rubber hose fed into each of the four burners and the hose led outside to a hundred-pound LP gas cylinder. When lit, the burners would throw a huge blue flame four feet in length, and once the squirrel cage fan started, enough heat was pushed into the tent to keep everyone toasty all night. The roar from the heater was deafening, so the entire contraption had to be kept outside the tent with only the opening protruding inside. The heater went through a hundred pounds of LP gas in ninety minutes. But that's how you heat a tent in winter.

Water was always a problem. Normally we dug trenches around the outside of the tent to catch rainwater. Sometimes we didn't get the trenches done soon enough, and water would come pouring into the tent. There were many nights when the inside of the tent looked worse than the outside. There would be ankle-deep mud everywhere. Sawdust and lime powder were the only practical ways to take care of the moisture, so we brought in sawdust and lime by the truckloads when we could find it.

One of the semi trailers acted as our stage. It was a large flat bed trailer with hinged sides each about eight feet high. When the sides let down, telescopic legs welded to the frame swung out to support them. Ramps and stairs were placed in front of the stage next and Astroturf carpeting was laid down in front for the penitents. Hundreds of wooden folding chairs were arranged in rows with a large center aisle down the middle. Four-foot-wide metal yokes containing mercury vapor lights were hoisted to the top of the tent using pulleys and winches. The book table was set up at the back and the band equipment was arranged on the stage, and we were ready for business. Offerings were collected in KFC chicken buckets.

The success of our preaching depended very much on the spiritual atmosphere of the city we were in. Some cities were great – the atmosphere at night in the tent was electric with anticipation. People would forget their cares, sing and clap and pray and flood to the front of the platform at the invitation. In other cities, very little would happen, and the meetings were a struggle every night. It was totally unpredictable. We never discovered a uniform formula for success. There was just something different about each city. Jesus discovered the same thing – there were cities where everyone listened and responded and then there were "Jerusalems" where He would be met with studied indifference.

We learned as soon as we started in India, that you don't need a tent. There simply wasn't a tent made that would have been able to hold all the people coming to those meetings. So we looked for parade grounds, cricket (the English version of baseball) fields or soccer fields for the use of our evangelistic meetings. During my time there, the average crowd per night was between 5,000 and 10,000 people. We were in the north of India. The earlier teams had seen crowds as large as 60,000 in south India.

A make-shift stage was built; steel poles were erected with fluorescent light fixtures on each pole; carpets were spread in front of the stage; rope lines were run to keep the crowd from getting too close to the stage; the sound equipment was hooked up and cranked to "10"; and the book table was filled with literature at the back of the grounds. Once this was done, we were in business and ready for the first night's meeting.

It's hard to describe what it's like speaking to that many people. Several things surprised me about them. First they sat on the ground. There simply was no way to procure that many chairs in any town, and the cost would have been prohibitive. But they were always totally content to sit cross-legged on the ground. Here they were, coming to hear me, a nobody from America, and were willing to sit there for more than two hours every night. It was very humbling.

I was also surprised by their attentiveness. Most of those attending were Hindu and Muslim yet they listened quietly and focused on every word in the message. The sheer size of the crowd was intimidating at first, but when I realized they were really listening to what I was saying, a comfort and confidence set in.

Next I was surprised by the response. We gave invitations almost every night much like a Billy Graham crusade in a U.S. stadium. People always came to the prayer area in front of the stage; hundreds of them. Our prayer workers always had their hands full. The post-meeting meeting often went as long as the regular meeting. Some came forward out of curiosity, some came for prayer due to sickness or family problems, some were bewitched, some were ready to surrender nasty habits and some came because they were ready to become Christ followers.

There were nights, after the preaching was over, that we asked the people to line up for prayer and come across the platform. Our team would also line up across the stage, and the people came through for prayer. We usually laid our hands on their heads and prayed very quickly as each one announced their particular need through an interpreter - 1,000 to 2,000 people waiting in line, so no dawdling! We often didn't get into bed until midnight or after. Preaching under those circumstances was one of the most exhausting things I've ever done, and on it continued, every night for six months.

Street Corner Preaching in India

Preaching on the streets in India had its hazards. First of all it was always hot, so we had to drink lots of fluids. Second the fluids available, such as the local water, were not always potable. Third the crowds considered the streets their turf, whereas the parade grounds were our turf. And being on their turf was definitely different.

We stopped our bus along side a highway one day near a small village in the state of Maharashtra. We sauntered into the village looking for a good place to preach and found a small street corner. One of the sisters acted as my interpreter, and we launched forth with a loud invitation for people to come hear us and receive our free literature. Shortly after I was finished, a couple of the village men approached us and asked if we would be willing to stay until that evening and give our presentation to the rest of the village. Most of the workingmen and women were out in the rice paddies that day and would be able to come that night.

Of course we were excited to be invited and agreed to the invitation, but asked about a place to have the meeting. One of the men said, "No problem, we've talked to the head priest (Hindu) in the village, and he's said it's all right if you use the temple tonight." I was skeptical and asked if we could go talk to this man, so we were led to his house.

As a matter of fact, it was okay with him, and we had our meeting venue for the evening. What I didn't know was that I had not just talked to the priest, but a man who thought of himself as the spokesman for the priest.

We arrived with our team of about 30 people that night and set up shop inside the Hindu temple. Most Hindu temples look like large gumdrops with a large stone and concrete porch surrounding the outside of the building. The place was packed that night as we began singing our Christian worship songs. I should have known something was wrong immediately when a strange, skinny little man in a loin cloth who looked like someone straight out of a Disney cartoon made his way to the front as we sang and began dancing a very strange dance in front of us, waving a lighted stick of incense as he gyrated about – Ben Gunn on Treasure Island. My interpreter, Linda, an Anglo-Indian, leaned over and whispered, "I think there may be trouble. Let's be careful about what we say."

Suddenly, after about three songs, all the lights in the village went out, and we were forced to wait for candles to light up the inside of the temple. Of course when the lights went out, so did our public address system, virtually guaranteeing the rest of the village could no longer hear what was being said inside the temple – this by design I think.

Susan, another Anglo-Indian team member, began to give her testimony about how Christ had changed her life, and midway through, Linda leaned over and said, "I think we better go."

I said, "Are you sure. The priest gave us permission to be here. Can't we just let Susan finish?"

Linda's eyes were wide by now and filled with a genuine fear – and she was not one to be afraid. And the weird little man continued his frenzied dance in front of us as the crowd cheered him on. "I just heard the men in the back call for the sticks," said Susan. "The Hindu priest has just arrived in the village and is inciting the village against us." Bringing out the sticks meant that four-foot-long cane sticks would be brandished by the village's strongest men, and we would be beaten and driven from the village.

I made an instant and extremely easy decision to retreat. Susan and Linda agreed. We thanked the crowd still gathered for their time and attention, and I turned to the team members and said, "Everyone head for the bus immediately!" The road out of the village to the bus seemed very long, but as we retreated, the lights of the village mysteriously came back on. Once on the bus, we were out of there in a heart beat and no one was injured. It turns out our little buddy, the priest's spokesman with whom we'd spoken earlier, wasn't even that; just some guy trying to look important. He never did show up at the temple that night. I think he was too busy manning the village light switches!

Chapter 29
Theatrical Preaching

Our main purpose in going places was to preach and share our witness of what Christ had done in our lives: street corners, homes, churches, tent meetings, bus stops, parade grounds, hospitals, prisons, on the telephone, night clubs, circuses, battleships, iron ore mines, television, radio, military bases, beaches, discotheques, university campuses, shopping centers – there really was no place we weren't prepared to go in order to carry out what we felt was our calling. We discovered that communicating the gospel could be done in many different ways and, indeed, Jesus varied his preaching approach wherever He went.

> "I am persuaded that the more open-air preaching there the better; if it becomes a nuisance to be a blessing to others—if properly conducted, if the Gospel is spoken, and if the spirit of the preacher is one of love and truth, the results cannot be doubted: The bread cast upon the waters must be found after many days. (Ecclesiastes 11:1.)

> As to style in preaching outdoors, it should certainly be very different from much of what prevails within, and perhaps if a speaker were to acquire a style fully adapted to a street audience, he would be wise to bring it indoors with him. A great deal of sermonizing may be defined as saying nothing at extreme length;

but outdoors verbosity is not admired. You must say something and have done with it and go on to say something more, or your hearers will let you know."

– from John Wesley, A Letter on Preaching Christ

Most of what we did on street corners had little effect on cities or groups of people. Street witnessing worked best one-on-one and many peoples' lives were touched that way. But for sheer emotional impact in the highways and byways, nothing could compare to our drama skits. I can't recall where we first came up with the idea of street drama, but I remember it was most effective in Europe and India. The only places where it worked in the U.S. were venues where people had gathered to party – we found that California and Florida beaches were perfect.

Newport Beach

Our most effective and widely used presentation was the crucifixion of Jesus. In some places, like India, we used very elaborate costumes and special effects. In other places, like California, we didn't need all that because the people knew exactly what we were doing. Newport Beach was such a place.

We were holding meetings in different locales in Orange County (Anaheim, Costa Mesa and Buena

Park), so we were fairly close to the beaches. We decided to put some costumes together (a few Roman soldiers, a blood-stained Jesus, mourning women) and took off for the most crowded beaches on the busiest afternoon in the middle of summer.

We began at one end of the beach near a huge pier. The drama team rode in a large van to the site, quietly exited the van and immediately the soldiers began driving Jesus through the crowds on the beach, heading south to where most of the activity was. The response from the crowd was amazing: mothers and children staring in disbelief; girls in bikinis shrieking and crying; jocks and surfers cursing and telling us to get out of there. But wherever the procession roamed along the beach, as Jesus was whipped, so also the crowd would whip up into a frenzied, very loud and very angry response. Here's what was weird, wherever we walked, the crowd parted for us. If you'd been in a helicopter looking down, you would have seen the crowd parting like the Red Sea for Moses.

When we arrived at our prime spot, the "soldiers" dug a hole in the sand, Jesus was thrown to the ground, fake wooden spikes were driven into his hands amid much yelling and screaming from the women mourning; and Jesus was hoisted up above the crowd, and the cross was deposited in the hole.

I can't explain the wonder of what happened next. It was as if we were all transported back in time to Golgotha. The atmosphere of blood lust and hatred for Jesus Christ was right there. Our girls, dressed up in their shrouds and robes, were not the only ones crying; many of the women, bikini-clad and half-drunk, were crying and sobbing as well, but not from mourning Jesus. They cried from shock and sheer, unbridled anger at us for having disturbed them in this way. They cursed us and told us to get out. "Who do you think you are coming here like this?" The macho boyfriends were equally outraged and threatened physical violence if we didn't leave. They all jeered at Jesus and us and shouted curses at these obnoxious "Jesus freaks" who had dared come to disrupt their frolic on the beach. And finally, the classic – a tanned, six-foot-tall, muscular kid walked up to Jesus, hanging there suffering on the cross, and offered him a beer! The crowd went absolutely nuts. He turned around, with beer hoisted high in the air, and the whole crowd raising their drinks as well and gave a yell in unison. It was surreal.

No better gospel could have been preached that day. Yes, half the crowd jeered, but not the other half. You could see their faces – reflection, soberness, maybe even conviction. Many of our crew, including me, were dressed normally – no costumes. We spent the rest of the afternoon going around to the sober-faced ones talking to them about eternal life and their spiritual condition. They listened and talked gently, thoughtfully, as if a switch had been flipped and the carnival had been exposed for what it was. We discovered that there's nothing quite like being brought face to face with the death of the Son of God to help a person, at least some persons, give careful thought.

The Crucifixion Goes on the Road

It went so well at Newport Beach that we decided to use drama in other places. We performed the crucifixion in downtown Helsinki, Finland to rave revues, especially from the police. They promptly arrested all of us, including Jesus, but not before quite a crowd in the city center saw Jesus die for their sins at rush hour.

Later we gave the same performance under the Eiffel Tower in Paris and were ushered to the police station. We had failed to understand that crucifixions could only take place with a proper street license. Who knew?

But the greatest reception was in India. We went all out. Elaborate costumes were assembled, horses were rented for the day for two of the Roman centurions, special packets of blood were prepared and announcements were made to the crowds many nights in advance that there would be a dramatic presentation of the crucifixion on the final night of the crusade. We had to emphasize "dramatic" because we found that many of the poor people simply could not distinguish between drama and the real thing. It was also an indication of how real we made it look

On the last night of the crusade (we did this in many cities), the horses and centurions appeared at the back of the crowd. By this night there were usually 7,000 to 10,000 people gathered. After a brief introduction from the platform, the procession through the crowd began. The response was incredible. As soon as people saw Jesus, covered in blood, crown of thorns, carrying his cross and being whipped by the Roman soldier as he stumbled along with the cross, they began weeping and shouting. Women would stand up and hold their hands in front of them wailing. Many of them would shout at the soldier and tell him to stop what he was doing. There were times when we wondered whether we were going to have to help our "Roman soldier" escape the anger of the crowd. It was, I think, much like it could have been in Jerusalem that day. For that matter, so was Newport Beach. I've never seen such a response to the gospel. As a result of this crucifixion drama, I began to understand what Paul the apostle meant by the "offense of the cross."

The Lady of Sin

Another street skit that brought real impact was our lady of sin. We dressed up one of our girls in a floor-length black robe, painted her hands and face white, accented her eyes with black makeup, frizzed her hair and colored it a spooky shade of gray. We dressed up other team members in different, every-day kind of dress: one was a businessman, another a doctor, another was a construction worker, another a prostitute, another a drug addict and we even had a priest thrown in for good measure. Then we attached each one to the "lady of sin" by a large towing chain. To the lady of sin we pinned signs that spelled out different sins in large, black letters – LUST, ADULTERY, GREED, CURSING, PRIDE, etc. Then the team began their trek through the city streets or along the beaches – anywhere it was crowded.

And as they went along, the "lady" would get right in people's faces and say, "I know who you are! I want you! I've got you! Did you know you're one of these? Why don't you come along with us?" And the people on the chain would exclaim to passersby: "Isn't it great to be free? Do your own thing, man! Me, a sinner? Impossible!" The prostitute would try to entice men to follow along. The drug addict would offer drugs. You get the point. Coming along behind them, our workers distributed tracts to people telling them how they might find true freedom in Christ. Again, we got very few indifferent reactions; it was always a shock fest.

The Funeral Procession

There was one skit that we could only pull off in Italy and was also very effective for its shock value. Funeral processions are very common in Italy, especially in rural areas. The coffin carrying the deceased is placed on a horse-drawn cart and wheeled through the town followed by a procession of mourners. They either go in procession to the local Catholic cathedral for the funeral or to the cemetery or both. We decided to try something similar.

Our carpenters made a coffin and painted it black. We procured a portable PA system powered by a 12-volt car battery. We rented a horse-drawn cart for the day. Early in the morning, we would place the coffin on the cart and surround the coffin with large flower arrangements. The flowers were an important part of the skit because they had to hide the loudspeakers from the PA system. A team member was dressed in a suit and laid down in the coffin. He was given a microphone that was attached to the PA system on the cart. The mourners all dressed in black, funeral dirges played through the onboard sound system and one of our brothers, who had actually been a Catholic priest, put on his vestments and led the cortege down the city streets. The ladies mourned and the men walked in solemn procession.

Again, the response from the people was amazing. Women on the streets would begin to weep, at times even following along to pay their respects. Men would remove their hats in respect. As we entered the Duomo square, (most major cities in Italy have a Duomo or cathedral near the city center), the procession stopped; there was a pause, and then, to everyone's shock and horror, the casket lid flew open and its occupant stood to his feet with microphone in hand and began preaching to the gathering crowd about Christ's resurrection from the dead.

No street drama in our repertoire generated more opposition than this one. One lady fainted on the street when the guy came out of the coffin. We had pastors who, when hearing we were coming to their city, begged us not to put on the funeral procession skit. It was that upsetting. But it really got the message across, and people understood exactly what we were talking about.

You might think this was unique, but it was not original. The Salvation Army, during its early days in Victorian London, often used street drama to accentuate its message. "You must say something and have done with it," wrote John Wesley, and there was no quicker way to pull this off than with drama.

Chapter 30
The Miracles

Until the visit to India, I had seen a handful, maybe, of what one could call healing miracles or healing events. I was not prepared for what was about to happen. I'd been told, but I remained skeptical; seeing was going to have to be believing.

It's probably a waste of time to argue whether miracles are for today's church or not. Theologians and ministers have debated this point for centuries with no conclusions drawn and very little common ground reached. All I can say is that when you go to the mission field, your theology about miracles ends up not meaning much.

We Americans live in a cultural bubble. Our materialism has robbed us, many times, of the ability to even be open to the possibility of any kind of supernatural breakthrough in a situation. What is common in third world countries in the area of spiritual activity is often considered wacky or nonsense here. "And why would we need miracles, anyway?" Westerners might ask. "We have science and sophisticated medicine. We have everything we need at our fingertips. We have knowledge and understanding of how things work in this world: the mapping of the human genome, intelligent computers, spacecraft on Mars, staggering breakthroughs in physics and biology."

Sophistication at that level quickly makes belief in miracles look more like medieval superstition. "Who needs miracles when you have reason and intelligence and technology?" The fact that this attitude has leaked into the church is a whole different discussion. Let's just say that even the church in the West struggles with the idea that God might just be able and willing to perform miracles, when necessary, through His children in certain situations.

Miracles became a way of life for us in the third world. It was not enough to just preach to the people. They could understand the preaching but only to a certain degree. One has to remember that these people did not grow up with Bibles or Sunday School or anything even remotely similar. They literally had no knowledge of Jesus. And so it was important to not only share the gospel, it was also important to show them, in practical ways, why it was good news. Often that is where miracles came in.

Of course most of the miracles Jesus performed had to do with healing. We also experienced many healing miracles. And it was through these miracles that the message of Jesus was passed on to other villagers and townsfolk. Once they'd heard about this from fellow villagers and family members, they would often come the next night; they wanted to see for themselves.

Doug had warned me before going to India that miracles would be a large part of our agenda in every city as the crusades opened. I had never seen major miracles like what he was describing, and I was a little fearful – "God, how in the world are you going to use me this way? I can barely exercise enough faith in You to take away a headache, let alone heal a blind man." I got no response from God, which is often His way of saying, "Relax and let me take care of it."

The Man with No Eyes

The first meeting on the first night in our first city in India also brought our first major miracle. He was the first man in line for prayer after we concluded the preaching that first night. He was more than blind – he had no eyes. He had been born with no eyes. The sockets were there, but there was nothing but pink tissue in the place of eyes. The counselors brought him to Doug and me, and I just kind of stared at Doug. "Now what?" I asked with a subdued, silly grin on my face. Doug looked down, shook his head in disbelief as if to say, "I knew this would happen," then opened his mouth in a half smile and just said, "Well, we'll have to pray. The whole crowd knows about this guy."

I was thinking, "This must be the devil's way of messing this meeting up right from the start. He's brought this man just to prove to the crowd that we're all a bunch of quacks." I reluctantly placed my hands on the man while Doug prayed and the team of counselors prayed and the worship team played behind us. Doug didn't waste much time praying. He knew better. He knew that when it came to miracles and hearing prayers for miracles, God wasn't deaf. He knew that if God was going to do something in this man, it would probably be done quickly, and he was right.

We backed away from the man and asked if he could see anything. To our amazement, he said he could see something like what would have been a shadow moving to us. Remember he had never seen, so it was impossible for him to describe much, since he had no experience of sight to relate to. That was all that happened that night – he could see shadows moving, but he could not see our fingers held up in the air. He could not count how many fingers Doug was holding up. We asked him to come back the next night, and he said he'd be the first one in line, and we knew he would be.

The following night, there he was, and up he came for his second installment of prayer. It was the same scene -–Doug looked at me, looked at the ground, half smiled and began to pray for him. He backed up from the man, held his hand in the air with three fingers extended and asked if he could count the fingers - "Three!" he said, very loudly (he did know how to count), followed by a ripple of murmurs and exclamations in the crowd. The amazing thing was that he could now see very well, and yet there were still no eyes in his eye sockets.

Raise the Dead

We were told not to travel in India at night, but when the first group arrived in 1976 many of them were naïve and careless and prone to scoff at local customs, even when they made sense. We had a small, old Mercedes Benz bus, which had made the trip to India from Europe. One night the team was traveling in the bus to the next town where meetings were to start the following day.

They came upon him before there was time to stop. In India, farming people travel on the major highways in oxcarts at night. The farmer just points the ox in the general direction he wants to go, and the ox seems to have enough intelligence to follow the highway. Then the farmer goes to sleep in the back of the cart since the trip usually takes all night anyway. They have no lights and no reflectors on the oxcarts, and that is one primary reason one does not drive at night in India.

This particular farmer was sound asleep when we caught up with him. When we collided, the ox, the oxcart and the farmer all went flying. When they landed, the ox and the farmer were both dead. We didn't bother with the ox's pulse, but we did have an RN with us, and she took the farmer's pulse, and there was none. So what do you do in the middle of India in the middle of the night with no hospital? Yes, you pray. The team leaders laid their hands on the poor man and asked God to bring him back. Instantly he sat up, looked around with a very surprised expression on his face and asked for a cup of coffee. We paid him for his ox and cart and took him to his destination. Had this man not revived, our bus driver would still be rotting in an Indian jail. We later learned from Westerners who had traveled in Asia that if you hit someone on a highway or have any kind of traffic accident, because you are a Westerner, you will automatically go to jail and only large amounts of cash will get you out. The policy they encouraged, which was difficult to accept, was: just keep on driving, get out of there as fast as you can and don't look back.

We did very little night driving in India after that.

In Miraj, a smaller town in Maharashtra but famous for its hospital which was started by Christian missionaries, two major miracles occurred during our meetings. Brahmins are high caste Hindus considered to be among the most devout of the many Hindu sects, (the caste system remains in place to this day in India) and a Brahmin priest attended our meetings one night. He had seen the crucifixion play we had presented and had wept through the whole thing according to a local missionary who knew him. The next day, the missionary was at my door. "Brother Joe, I need to see you. The Brahmin priest has asked if you would be willing to visit his sick wife in the hospital. He is desperate for a cure for her, she's been to doctors everywhere (both M.D.s and witch doctors) and nothing has worked. Can you come?"

This poor woman had an issue of blood that had afflicted her for six years. No one could help her, and everyone knew she might die if not healed. We went to her hospital room. She was very weak and very pale; her relatives and her husband surrounded us. It was sad. Here were two of the most well to do people in that city, respected by everyone, and yet there was literally nothing that could be done for her. We anointed her head with oil, then I prayed and my Norwegian friend interpreted. We tried to offer words of encouragement to the family and invited them back to the meeting that night.

Late that afternoon, shortly before we went to the meeting grounds, word came through the missionary that as soon as we left the hospital, the woman's bleeding stopped. By next morning she had regained her strength and was dismissed from the hospital with no bleeding – the first time it had stopped in six years. Both man and wife were in the meetings during the remainder of our stay in Miraj but we would never know the long-term impact on their lives.

Another miracle happened a few nights later. People were finding it too difficult to come to our crusade grounds, so they asked for a one-night meeting near a squatter's section in a poor neighborhood. They had heard about the miracles happening at the crusade grounds near the Christian-run hospital and wanted to bring their sick for prayer.

The first woman in the line that night had carried her twelve-year-old son from her shack several blocks away so we could pray for him. He was paralyzed from his waste down and had been for nine years. I asked her to set him down in front of me while a couple of others supported him under his arms, and the whole crowd watched silently. As soon as I prayed for him, we could see a change. I asked him if he felt any different, and he said, "Yes." Then I asked him to try to take a step or two. He took several. At first he had trouble getting his legs and feet to work. Walking was something he had never done. But by the end of the night, he was not only walking back and forth, he was taking an occasional leap.

It was like this in every place in every meeting – hundreds, sometimes thousands, of people waiting in line for prayer or inviting us to their homes or hospitals to only pray: "Please pray for us; we've heard what God can do." In other words, "You have a hotline to a God we've never heard of, and can you speak with Him on our behalf." It's strange – I rarely felt a tingle or premonition or buzz or surge of energy or faith when I prayed for these precious ones. We were so tired most of the time; drained from the heat and stress of the physical situation, it was hard to feel anything. After praying for hundreds it was too difficult to pray loudly (as in, "Ok, I really mean it this time.") or pray with extra emphasis or earnestness; it seems our physical and emotional weakness made excellent power conduits for God.

Tent revival meetings birthed through the Pentecostal movement in the South during the first half of the twentieth century were known for their emotional, ecstatic displays accompanied by shouts, praises, visions, prophecies, people falling over, shaking and jerking. It was and still is quite a scene. None of that happened in India; the music played, our team sang choruses but that was the extent of the display. We discovered that God doesn't need cheerleaders, just availability. We showed up for the meetings, prayed by laying our hands on their heads as Christ instructed his disciples and it seems God did the rest.

There are many other stories to tell about our miracle experiences in India, and I know my fellow teammates can tell them. Miracles were an every day occurrence, one after another every night, especially healing miracles. India is still a place where God works in supernatural ways and shows Himself to these wonderful people. As a pastor friend of mine used to say: "God does surprising things with surprising people in surprising ways, so don't be surprised!"

Chapter 31
On to The Philippines

We stayed in India for six months; six action-packed, non-stop, scary and heart-warming months. Our visas ran out and we made plans for our next destination – The Philippine Islands. Christ is the Answer already had an evangelism team located on the islands (they had begun there while we were in India), but they were due for a leadership change and, since we were on that side of the world, Gayle and I were selected.

Like most of our postings in those days, we were sent forth with much good will and very little cash. I think we arrived in Manila with $40. We found a missionary house run by the Christian and Missionary Alliance Church, settled our things there and began wondering what to do next. Our group of fellow disciples who had begun ministry just north of Manila had returned to the States by that time so it was up to us to fend for ourselves. Our CMA friends at the guesthouse made some calls and contacted another group in Quezon City, the twin city to Manila, and we moved to their dormitories with not much left of our $40.

I remember our first night in Manila – Gayle and I decided to take a trip to the city center in search of a Pepsi. Weird – we had no access to American-made anything in India and we were longing for a taste of The West. So here we were, back in civilization – a taxi ride downtown in a Toyota, three Pepsis and a taxi ride home. It didn't take much to make us happy after feeling the isolation of India.

Isolation – I think that's what separates real missionaries from wannabe's. Real missionaries, we discovered, could handle isolation from their familiar culture for long periods of time; their new environment became their environment, their new home, their new reality. Lifelong missionaries to third world places seemed comfortable with the culture quirks, the new language and food, the rhythm of a life totally foreign from what we knew in America or Europe. I didn't realize this until we tried it ourselves and, as a result, developed great respect for them. I didn't want to sound like a spoiled American so I never had a serious discussion with a missionary about how they had overcome separation anxiety; but it was obvious from their tenures in their respective countries that they no longer felt isolation. The missionary to India had become Indian. The missionary to The Philippines had become a Filipino. He didn't miss Pepsi.

Our new hosts in Quezon City were part of a Pentecostal mission, Christ to the Philippines. They had done an incredible work over the years establishing a home church in Quezon City along with a Bible school and then sending out their young graduates to plant churches in the towns and villages from which they had come. All of our dorm mates were Filipinos either helping with the Bible school or the church or in transition and soon to be sent out to start new churches. They were wonderful young adults and families; always smiling, always ready to serve us and deeply devoted to God and His kingdom expansion.

The Philippines consists of over 7,000 islands spread in a north-south line off the coast of China in the South China Sea. The national language is Tagalog (tuh–gah'–log) but most people we met in towns and cities spoke English and were excited to meet Americans. Kids and adults in the market places and on the streets would shout out "Hey Joe!" At first I was wondering how they knew my name until I found out that every American since World War II was "Joe" – that is what they called our soldiers then and became every American's moniker after that. Our troops had freed them from the Japanese and had endured horrendous casualties and hardships in doing so, and they never forgot it, evidenced by the greetings even to us.

Filipinos, although seemingly exuberant and bold when with friends on the street, were extremely shy one to one. We learned the oriental principle called "hya" from our missionary friends. Basically it means, "I am ashamed to you," a term of deference and humility expressed toward those you do not know. It was very difficult to adjust our bold, in-your-face approach American-style to the "shame" of the Filipino. I lost count of the number of times I tried getting a response from a shopkeeper or pedestrian or church member when I had what I thought was a legitimate question.

"Which way to the bus stop?" I would ask.

"Just that way," was the response with a head bob in the general direction.

I tried to get the person to be more specific – "Is it a block that way or four blocks that way?"

The hand would go to the mouth, an embarrassed smile would ensue and absolutely no eye contact – at first it made me crazy, so much so that I would get irritated thinking the person to be messing with me or being rude on purpose. It was not that; not at all. It was their way of demonstrating embarrassment (shame) at having to be asked twice, and the more I asked or insisted on clarity, the more the person would withdraw or shut down. The response in every situation was without exception. One simply did not insist on getting vital information from a person he did not know.

We were cautioned about greeting others, especially man to woman – no handshakes or hugs. Shaking a woman's hand, at least a woman with whom I was not acquainted, was, in Filipino culture, equivalent to a marriage proposal. I must have had women going home telling their parents the good news every other day. We were cautioned to never look a person in the eye as we were speaking – in their culture that was the social equivalent of a challenge to one's honor. And on it went – learning the nuances and anathemas of a new people in a new land; we tested the patience of many a Filipino and probably offended many.

We could not have met up with better people than the Christ to the Philippines couples. It wasn't long before word had gotten out that we were there to go into rural places to hold evangelistic meetings and to pray for the sick and hopefully plant new churches in those areas. Our mission dovetailed perfectly with their mission and soon we met the regional pastor for the southern Bicol region, Sinforoso Tindugan.

Pastor Tindugan was a number of years older than I was but came to serve in any capacity. A few Americans had been in his district but not many and none had been willing to do the kind of meetings we were planning. We made the necessary connections and to his enthusiastic invitation found ourselves heading to the southern part of the main island of Luzon to Naga City, Pastor T's hometown and operating base.

Our first trip to the Bicol region was an adventure unlike anything we'd yet experienced. We loaded into a small bus in Cubao, Quezon City with all of our earthly possessions: Gayle, Amie and me. The luggage went on top and everyone else, 50 people in a bus designed for 25, crammed inside. Amie, still our little 2-year-old charmer, charmed her way into a seat. She sat on Gayle's lap while I stood. It was a long trip, and I don't remember much except the maniacal velocity at which the bus plunged down the two lane highway, the curves and bumps and passing slower-moving trucks with horns, the loudest horns I had ever heard, blaring at oncoming vehicles as if the sound alone would knock them out of our way. Painted on the back of every truck were two arrows: one pointing left that read "Passing Side" and one pointing right that said, "Suicide." I wondered, "Why would commercially-licensed drivers need someone to tell them which side was for passing?"

Gayle, Amie and I became the Christ is the Answer Philippines pioneer team. We'd gained a foothold in the country and were now in Naga City and getting ready for our first open air meetings in small towns to the south of Naga. Four other Americans had now joined us and, with our six plus Pastor Tindugan and young people from his church, we launched out holding our first meetings in town squares with a cheap string of lights and a battery-operated sound system. Our Filipino friends would lead the singing, Gayle and I would throw in a couple American tunes, I would preach, Pastor T would interpret and we began seeing results. The attendance numbers were nothing like what they had been in India, but the receptivity to our message was enthusiastic.

The Philippines is predominantly Roman Catholic having first been visited in 1521 by Ferdinand Magellan and settled in 1565 by Miguel López de Legazpi, both men being Spanish emissaries, naming the islands in honor of King Philip II of

Spain. As a result many people, towns and cities still carried Spanish names and Spanish was still spoken and understood in some areas. Although Catholic in name, we discovered that religious practice in most towns and villages was syncretistic – a mixture of pagan belief with Catholic belief. Witch doctors, sorcerers, astrologers and such made a very good living among less-educated people and non-Catholic rituals bordering on outright witchcraft frequently accompanied the Catholic festivals. The deeper we penetrated into villages and jungle areas, the more pronounced the practices and, where prevalent, presented increased hostility to our message of Jesus Christ, the one Savior. In one village a church was known for its "Black Maria" where a black statue of Mary wept tears of blood. The priest of that church condemned our presence in the village and people were warned not to attend our meetings or face excommunication. Mary wept. I think.

If you travel in the Philippines, you have four choices – jeepneys, buses, airplanes and boats, boats being the preferred means of travel because of the numerous islands making up the archipelago. Jeepneys were Willys Jeeps procured from World War II American leftovers. The chassis was lengthened to accommodate a longer bed, benches running the length of the bed were added and a canopy to shelter the passengers completed the transformation. The old gas engines were removed and Isuzu four-cylinder diesels were installed along with a wild palette of colors, lights and a blaring sound system. We stayed primarily on the main island of Luzon but after moving 200 miles south of Manila to Naga, we discovered land transportation, which we had been using up to that time, wouldn't be enough. We were surrounded by ocean, and the villages we wanted to reach were often only accessible by water.

So we wrote to our prayer partners in the States for a boat. Boats in the Philippines are not fancy. The "banca" is little more than a hollowed-out mahogany log with sides built up using quarter inch marine plywood and vertical bracing. Ours was about 40 feet long and no more than three feet wide in the middle. The bow and stern narrowed down to points like a canoe. Outriggers are, of course, necessary. Without them, these boats would sink in no time in the high seas. The outriggers are made of bamboo poles about three inches in diameter extending out about ten feet from each side of the boat. One lies perpendicular across the front end and one across the back. Another bamboo pole on each side connects the two crosswise poles at their ends. These are the actual outriggers, and they plane along in the water parallel to the boat keeping it steady.

Bancas are powered by inboard, single-piston Briggs and Stratton engines. Most of the fishermen we knew had ten horsepower rigs, but we wanted more speed, so we got a sixteen. The engines are fastened to the bottom of the canoe toward the rear, and a long, stainless steel shaft runs out the stern from the back of the engine. A propeller is attached to the end of the shaft, and you're all set to go.

Our "banca" was a work of art. We were the envy of all the fishermen in Pasacao, our home port, but we hadn't taken her on a voyage. Levi, one of our Filipino leaders, was from the town of Ragay to the north of Pasacao. There were only two ways to get to Ragay – train and boat. We decided to take both. We sent Gayle and some of the Americans on ahead to Ragay by rail, and the rest of us, about ten people, prepared the boat.

Our guide was Pastor Belen. He was a fisherman in a small village near Ragay and said he knew the waters well. Our first mistake was believing Pastor Belen. Our second mistake was allowing him to convince us to leave Pasacao at two in the afternoon. But we set sail anyway.

I have to say it was absolutely exhilarating to be cutting through the smooth, emerald-green ocean water, watching the flying fish and mackerel jumping on either side and enjoying the breath-taking scenery as we tooled along parallel to the coast line about a mile offshore. I hadn't a care in the world, and the boat was running like a fine-tuned machine.

But the sun began to sink in the west, and we were still two hours from Ragay. Belen said he knew of a short cut that would get us to his village quicker. We could spend the night in his home, and head into Ragay in the morning. The "shortcut" was a small river that cut through a rather large peninsula that jutted out into the Ragay Gulf. It was common for fishermen in his area, he said, to use the river when they were in a hurry to get home. Adriano, our captain, steered us toward the river as Belen stood up on the bow directing him. The sun had set, and we were left with very little light to navigate. We eased into the inlet of the river and immediately hit the sandy bottom of the river. We weren't going anywhere.

It was then that Belen remembered something important. It was low tide. He never went down this river at low tide. It was impassable and impossible. We had one option – head the boat back out to sea a ways and continue on around the peninsula, which is exactly what we did. We were pretty much navigating in the dark now, with no instruments, no compass, no lights and a storm brewing offshore. Adriano gave it full throttle, Belen still standing in the bow squinting in the dark making sure our path was clear so we'd make good time and get in before the storm hit.

About ten minutes into our new route it happened – there was a thud, then a long scraping sound along the bottom of the boat, and we tipped to one side going full speed ahead. Out port outrigger dipped down into the water and immediately shattered. Things began spilling out into the ocean as people screamed and held on. The Filipino girls who were along to help us could not swim. Our pilot, Adriano, saved our lives. As soon as we hit the coral reef, he leaped into the air like a trapeze artist, grabbed onto the starboard outrigger, which was now sticking straight up in the air and his weight brought the boat back to its proper attitude in the water. We had no port outrigger. It was floating away in the open sea having broken off from the impact against the reef. Yes, Belen had forgotten again – a double error. Not only was the river impassable at low tide, but this reef was as well.

Allen Ols, my right-hand man, and I jumped into the water to retrieve the severed outrigger, cutting our feet on the coral as we swam around. We found it, brought it back to the boat, and Adriano and Levi began lashing it to the boat again with some nylon line we'd found. We stabilized the boat by holding onto the sides while we were in the water until the outrigger was fastened back on. Then it was safe to crawl back in.

In the meantime, Adriano had succeeded in re-starting the engine, but the propeller and shaft were all but useless having been bent on the hard, coral reef. We tried inching ahead, but it was useless. More coral stretched out ahead of us, and it was night. We couldn't tell if there was five feet of coral or five miles of coral ahead of us. We were a couple of miles from shore and not another boat in sight. The wind was beginning to stir and there was lightning in the clouds directly behind us. All I could see in my mind was our little boat disintegrating on the coral reef as the waves from the storm began to build. I bowed my head and, in my heart, prepared to die. Everyone grew quiet and somehow I summoned the grace to lead a prayer for everyone. We committed ourselves to God and asked Him for wisdom what to do. Adriano suddenly had a wild idea.

We backed the boat up as far as we could off the reef, managed to turn the bow around straight out to the ocean and headed out into the bay in four-foot waves. The rain and storm were now on us full strength. For a while, Al and Levi stayed in the water, hanging onto the side of the boat to help stabilize us as we crippled forward. The thump, thump of the propeller shaft was frightening, but it was our only hope. We spent the next half hour negotiating the deep water out from the peninsula and eventually got around it.

About the time the storm ended, we hit shallow water and found we could touch bottom, so we cut the power and took turns walking the boat toward Belen's village by the bay. We arrived after midnight, hauled ourselves up to his bamboo cottage and collapsed on the floor. I've never been so happy to be on dry ground.

The next morning Belen's wife woke us all up as she fixed breakfast and chattered at Belen non-stop. Levi translated for us later. "Why did you take them through there at night? You knew better than to come that way. You knew these are shark-infested waters, and that people have died out there!" We also found out the reef was called the "enchanted reef," because so many people had lost their lives on it. I thought about our bleeding feet dangling down below the boat the previous night, and I realized who was watching out for us.

Chapter 32
Culinary Adventures

The typical day-to-day staple for most Filipinos was rice with fish and vegetables. And that's what we had 90% of the time. It was usually pretty tasty, although we had to get used to the vegetable and fish being cooked in coconut milk. Filipinos take ripe coconuts, break them open, dump the milk into the cooking pot and then shred the remaining meat of the coconut. After shredding, the meat is squeezed through a strainer to remove any remaining liquid and is then added to the pot. Then the shredded coconut is thrown away or fed to the hogs. We Americans, accustomed to our Christmas macaroons and coconut cream pie, could not understand why. At first we strongly objected to the waste coconut shreddings, but were laughed at so much we gave in after awhile and just pitched it to the hogs like the locals.

But there were interesting things they ate which we had never seen. This is where the shock value of their food came into the picture. Chicken's feet were grilled over open charcoal at street stands in every city. That was a particular delicacy. If you weren't into the feet you could also get chicken gizzards on a stick that were grilled the same way.

With so many fish in the markets, it was common on our table. The preferred part of the fish, though, for the Filipino is the head. Our team members would fight over who got the head, the brains and the eyes. We always let them have ours! It wasn't something we felt warranted our competition.

Balut (bah – loot') is the favorite national treat in the Philippines. Balut is a duck egg with a duck embryo already forming inside. The egg is boiled and salted and sold at bus stands and in the market places. Filipinos simply peal the shell and eat the duck embryo feathers and all. That's right, the secret is cooking the egg just before the duckling is ready to hatch! I was never able to work up the courage or the desire to eat balut much to the chagrin of my Filipino friends.

I ate my first octopus and squid in the Philippines. It's actually very tasty and is cooked in the ink, which they squirt behind them when threatened.

One time we were on the small island of Burias and were staying in a small village with a fisherman and his family. He was also the pastor of the only evangelical church on that island. A side note, we were the first white faces people had seen on this island since World War II. One day the pastor asked if we wanted to go fishing with him. Well, we had our banca and he had his, so why not?

We headed about a half-mile off shore to a beautiful coral reef. Facing the boats stern to stern, we took one end of his five-foot-wide net and slowly pulled away from each other as he fed more of the net to us. We made a huge circle with the net finally joining him at the end of the circle thus making a

226

kind of fish corral with the stretched-out net. It was probably a hundred feet in diameter.

Next he told everyone in the boats to jump in the water and to splash and swim around as much as possible. I asked him if there were sharks on this reef, and he said at times there were, but that they wouldn't bother anyone. I thought about that as I splashed and frolicked in the water. The local kids gave us small goggles, so we could see more clearly underwater. And what I saw under that water took my breath away. I've never seen such beauty anywhere in any part of the world. The fish were iridescent – blues and yellows and reds and purples and greens – a beauty on display that would have taken my breath away only I was under water and inhaling was not permitted. The coral background, and the beautiful plants and seaweed gently swaying and the various other creatures – starfish, urchins and sea horses – I wanted to stay there the rest of my life and just look. Never has God's infinite creative power stood out to me as it did that day.

When it was time to get out of the water, he gave the signal and his kids started helping him pull in the nets. The catch was amazing. The nets were full of what we know as needlefish in the U.S. A needlefish is a sort of anorexic barracuda (or for you Wisconsin sportsmen, a musky). The needle in needlefish comes from its many sharp, protruding teeth. It comes in various sizes although the typical one in our nets that day was about two feet long. We hadn't seen them in the water, but evidently when we had splashed about, they got stuck in the nets as they tried to escape.

The village was delighted upon our return. We shared the fish with as many people as we could and had an incredible meal that night. The fish were cut up cross-wise into steaks and had very few bones. What bones there were turned blue when cooked so it was easy to see them and pick them out. The fish tasted like fine tuna; our best meal by far during our stay on the islands, this on an island with no electricity, no telephones, no plumbing and only wood stove cooking. Amazing.

Siegfried

Siegfried Echelas was our cook. "Siggy" had been a professional cook on board luxury cruise ships based out of Manila and Sydney, Australia. He had also been a pimp and a Communist guerrilla. He met us in Santo Domingo in Albay province. Our evangelism team was holding meetings there in sight of the famous Mayon volcano, a perfectly shaped cone volcano that was and is still active. Each morning we would wake up to this incredible sight out of our bedroom window - a constant plume of smoke coming out of the top of a mountain forty miles away that could wreak devastation in a very short period of time when aroused.

Siggy came to the meetings one night and gave his heart to Christ. He left Santo Domingo and traveled with us, becoming, by default, our cook. Siggy could make absolutely delicious meals out of nothing. The only problem was that often he would refuse to disclose what that "nothing" was he was serving. One afternoon we had a wonderful meal with an unusual tasting meat entrée. It was delicious, just unusual. We prodded him for a couple of days trying to get him to tell us what it was, and finally he confessed to serving us dog! Come to think of it, we never once saw a stray dog in the Philippines.

Eating in other countries was something we simply adjusted to; sometimes it was a great experience and sometimes it was quite unpleasant. The extent of my knowledge of Indian food went to one word: curry. I didn't know, really, what they ate nor had I much interest. Our trip to India brought all kinds of new surprises, including the food.

Calling Indian food spicy is being polite. "Fire" is a better word. "Inferno" also comes to mind. It's basically the same in Pakistan. On our way through to India, we stopped in Islamabad, the capital city, and Doug treated us all to shami-kabab. Shami-kabab is nothing more than a glorified hamburger made from ground goat meat. It's served with flat bread, not on a bun. But it's not the goat meat or the appearance that makes this dish different. It's what they put in the goat meat that's so special.

The meat is saturated with white-hot chilies, the hottest little green things I've ever tasted. After a few bites, the shami-kabob begins to catch up to you. Your throat begins to constrict, and your tongue goes numb with pain. We thanked Doug for the experience and drank water for the next few hours.

Food in India was no different. Curries and cooking oils and lentils and vegetables were all mixed with generous helpings of chilies. It was very hot. But after we were in India for a while, we began to develop a taste for their food. We still love it.

Indian restaurants were unusual and at times bordered on the absurd. First we had to adjust to the fact that, no matter the location, no matter the sophistication of the restaurant, we would be dealing with live critters crawling around, either large roaches or large rats, but they almost always joined us for our restaurant meals.

In a small town in southern India, two of our girls had to use the restroom during a meal at one small roadside restaurant. The way to the restroom was through the kitchen. As they went through, they noticed the window opened to the back of the restaurant and there, hanging their huge heads inside the kitchen, were two Brahma bulls. The cooking pots and dirty plates from customers had been placed neatly on a table right under the back window, and the cows were helping themselves, licking the pots and plates clean. The girls looked around and saw no dishwater or soap anywhere – and they all wondered about the meal they had just eaten.

Eat With Your Right Hand!

We had to take toilet paper with us to India. It exists there, but not in abundance and only in the bigger cities. "So what do you do?" one might ask. Well, sometimes we forked out lots of money and bought Indian toilet paper, but it was more like sandpaper and practically unusable. The next worse thing was that you couldn't flush the Indian stuff down the toilet! It would clog the sewer system, and then there would really be a mess. So we were left with one option – get used to doing things the Indian way. One had to use one's left hand!

Now although this sounds gross, it's really not too bad. Once we got used to it, there were no complaints, and it became a normal routine of daily life. As a matter of fact, it helped explain why we were always seeing people in India heading out to the forests and empty fields each morning with a little can of water and then returning – the morning constitutional.

The only real complication from all of this was, of course, the fact that one eats with one's hand in India. Not only was there very little toilet paper in India, there were very few eating utensils. As a matter of fact, eating with one's fingers was and is a way of life. A pile of rice was dumped in the middle of the plate and small metal cups of curry, dal (curried orange lentils), and spiced-up vegetables were placed on the outside rim of the plate next to the rice; and then six-inch-diameter flat bread called chapatti. The custom was to tear off a piece of the chapatti, dip it in the curry, surround some rice with this mixture and pop the whole thing in your mouth. For those more advanced, a little curry was poured over the rice; the rice/curry mixture was worked into a small ball, held in the palm, brought to the mouth and popped in with the thumb.

This all had to be done with the right hand ONLY! The left hand had been used for hygienic purposes that morning, hence right-handed eating. This took some practice. Yes, we always washed our hands after our toilet experience; but still, in public, if one was eating Indian-style, one never, never ate with the left hand.

Supper with an Arabian Prince

One of our most interesting meals was not taken with Indians. We were in the aforementioned city of Miraj, which was, as I said, the home of a very famous missionary hospital. It was a little like the Mayo Clinic here in the States. People from all over Asia went there if they needed truly professional care and couldn't find help anywhere else. Evidently word had spread throughout the Middle East and there were frequent visitors from places like Saudi Arabia and Kuwait. One such man was visiting the Miraj hospital during our stay. He was from the oil-rich state of Qatar and was unbelievably wealthy: an oil sheik who had heart problems and had come to Miraj for specialized care.

We saw him one day outside his rented house near where we were staying. One of our guys made friends, and the sheik asked to meet our group's leader (me at that time). We were invited to a special noon meal, which in Qatar was the main meal of the day.

At the meal, he wore the typical Arab garment – a long, white robe, black leather sandals, a red calico head covering held in place by a type of rope device which looked like a sophisticated, three-tier headband. He had not come to India alone; he had an entourage – brothers, children, his wife (whom we never saw) and his mother-in-law (whom we never saw). The two women did all the cooking.

We were invited into a small living room in the front of his house, which had almost no furniture. We all sat down in the middle of the room cross-legged, and a large white sheet was spread before us. Onto that sheet was dumped the largest pile of rice I had ever seen, at least a foot tall and three feet in diameter. Onions and various other vegetables were brought out and then the main course, roast mutton. We each had a "plate" in front of us fashioned from dried banana leaves, and we helped ourselves to the pile of rice and all the mutton we could eat. It was fabulous.

He shared with us about his many physical problems. He was very rich. He had a huge mansion in Qatar; his sons each had their own bedrooms, each one with its own TV. He could own whatever car he wanted. Yet here he was in a Christian-run hospital with Christian doctors and nurses who would gather each morning before treating patients to have prayer together. I'm sure they prayed for this Muslim sheik. We did, too. He asked us for prayer after the meal, but we never saw him again.

Chapter 33
Adventures in Paradise

Once out of Manila, it's easy to see why The Philippines could be referred to as a tropical paradise. It is everything one thinks of: tall, swaying palm trees loaded with coconuts, endless beautiful beaches, coral reefs ablaze with a neon spectrum of colors and shapes; amazing to the eye and to the imagination and replete with photo opportunities for travel posters. And then there was the Philippines in real life; the place into which we had been introduced in order to bring the hope of life, real life, to Filipinos living out the nitty gritty just like billions of others all over the world.

Our meetings were usually well-attended as I mentioned earlier; townspeople, curious more than anything, checking it out just so they could see and meet the white-skinned Americans who had shown up out of the blue. Amie was a huge hit, the "walking doll" as she was often called. The Filipino girls traveling with us would sweep her away in the morning and run out into the village so she could meet the village kids. She was irresistible. Rumors flew through one village that a goddess had re-appeared. According to the village folklore, a goddess with white skin and bleached white hair had once lived there and brought very good luck. When they saw Amie, they couldn't believe it: a reincarnation of the goddess from long ago. She was swarmed and almost worshipped. The difficulty in this kind of popularity was that children and women showed their affection by touching and pulling her hair and pinching her chubby cheeks – painful. After awhile we had to monitor Amie's forays into the villages so she could recover.

Most of our meetings in the Philippines were in the open air. Since it is a small country with limited open space, we were usually forced to use the town squares or "plazas" for our meetings. There wasn't much going on, and it was fairly easy to procure the permits necessary to use the plazas. Lights were strung out and the sound equipment was prepared, and we were ready to go. Each plaza normally had its own stage, so that made things much easier.

The people were invited to attend during the day. We went house-to-house distributing leaflets announcing the meetings. Since we were the only white people many of them had seen in years, they came out of curiosity more than anything else at first. I preached through an interpreter, and we prayed for the sick each night. The response was wonderful.

Because of political tensions, we had to be careful in a few places. Communist guerrillas would come down from the mountains at night to check us out. We didn't know who they were exactly, but the people knew them. As a result, there were times when the plaza would be lined with army or police personnel for our protection. There had been kidnapping of Westerners.

One night in Sorsogon, a young man in the crowd hurled a fist-sized rock at me while I preached. He missed me and hit my assistant, Al, right in the head, knocking him out and creating quite a fuss. We took Al to the local police station, the doctor showed up and nursed his head, and he eventually regained his senses. The perpetrator was apprehended in the mean time and was brought straight to the police station to confront us. The police asked us what we wanted to do with him, and Al just said, "Tell him that I forgive him and that Jesus loves him – that we want him to know the Lord in his heart and to be at the meeting tomorrow night." I can't remember if he was there or not, but it was several days before Al's black and blue head was back to normal.

It was common to pray for people after the preaching was finished, sometimes a hundred or more, and they brought all kinds of disease and weakness to us for prayer. During our first meeting in San Pascual on Burias Island, a young lady brought her grandfather up front. The family lived a long distance away and the grandfather had been paralyzed and could not walk with them to the meetings. So the young lady had hired a fisherman to bring them from their village in a boat. They had arrived early and had waited a long time for the meetings to start.

Allen met with the grandfather and granddaughter after we were finished. I was so tired from preaching that I'd already gone home to bed. But as

Allen prayed for this old man, strength began to come back into his legs. He began to walk for the first time in years and even walked back to his village that night, through the jungle with his daughter! The next night half their village came back with them to the meetings. The demonstration of God's power worked.

I hesitate to say that God used the miracles to draw people but that was a legitimate and welcome by-product. Crowds followed Jesus everywhere He went once they'd witnessed the healings for themselves; so it was with us. But crowds also deserted Jesus when the time came for truth telling, because men are fickle creatures: we are attracted to the dazzle but distracted if the dazzle begins penetrating too deep. Mostly I believe Jesus healed people at our meetings for the same reason He always heals: it's because He loves us. Healing is a demonstration of God's compassion, period.

Chapter 34
Typhoon

Hurricanes in The Philippines are called typhoons. We'd never been through a typhoon and did not know what to expect. Our Filipino mates didn't talk about it much. A big one hit while we were staying in Naga City between meetings. We all knew something was up because winds had picked up and people had begun to stock up for a couple of days' worth of food. The Filipinos on our team prepared by not only stocking up but by nailing the shutters to the windows so they could not flap about.

The storm surge was much more than we expected – a wall of wind and rain that was more than momentary, lasting hours. We huddled on the second story of the house in whatever dry place we could find. Even with shutters nailed, the wind forced rain through every crack spraying water like a power washer. Winds of 100 mph and more were sustained, not intermittent, and at times we wondered if the cinder block house was going to hold steady.

After a night and a day, huddled together in our ark, the storm passed, the winds calmed and we peered out to see what had happened. The sight was horrible – every banana tree in the neighborhood (there were many, since people often grew their own in order to feed their own) had either been flattened or blown away completely; palms hung broken in half and limp; roads were still covered with water and many shacks in the neighborhood had simply disappeared, blown away into the surrounding jungle. We hoped that the people had found other shelter. The first floor of our house that contained the kitchen, dining hall and shower was completely flooded. As the water drained away into the afternoon the guys found many fish stranded on the floor – a food byproduct of the hurricane.

The weather was always unpredictable wherever we went. We always had to rely on the local fishermen to let us know whether it was safe to venture out with the boat. There were days when we were ready to set sail, beautiful sun and gentle winds, and they would warn us not to go; something they'd seen in the moon the night before. They were never wrong.

Epilogue

We stayed in the Philippines for a year and returned to the U.S. in March 1980, having planted and sustained for that year and proving that our style and our method were viable. I'm very happy and proud to say that that ministry as well as the tent ministry in Italy and in other countries have survived and thrived over the years and still operate in both places. It is all of God's grace, of course, but it is the men and women with whom we partnered in those early years that made things happen and were God's hand extended to the population. We ventured into some pretty dark places and sometimes came away with very little. But, as I quoted at the beginning, "A ship in harbor is safe - but that is not what ships are for."

The years since the close of the decade I've just chronicled have calmed somewhat, the adventures less dramatic. We all mature and eventually move into our life's groove. I have been a pastor since 1986 and enjoy the challenge and enjoy teaching and mentoring others who have embarked on their own faith journey. I have to say that much of what I teach is what not to do, since my failures far outweigh my victories. The bravado of youth is tempered over the years; the man is broken and crushed by life, circumstances, mistakes, poor judgment, misinterpretation, betrayal and failed relationships. One goes to the brink often, expecting never to recover.

What has sustained me is that Gayle has been at those brinks by my side – unbelievable mercy, unspeakable sacrifice, unbreakable will – having decided to make the journey with me. One could not ask for a better partner.

Some plant, some water, but God, according to Paul, gives the increase and provides the harvest. Most of the stories have yet to be told. What you've read here is a micro-account; ten years of our lives. Many of our friends continue the work in those places having spent decades in the trenches. My hope is that, as you've read, you've been inspired and maybe challenged to see what God can do in you. All he needs is permission. He waits for your signal. C.T. Studd wrote, "What God wants is hot, willing hearts; any old turnip will do for a head." My problem is not my turnip; it's my heart, my will, my availability. What you've read about all of us in this book is the account of willing individuals, not qualified individuals; people who made themselves available. Credentials, from what we read in the Bible, seem to be down the list. A person's qualification, actually, has already been determined if he meets the prerequisites: believe, be baptized, go.

Think about it. Pray about it. Ask God what He might have for you. Get ready for the adventure – it is beyond your wildest imagination!

The Beat Goes On!

Many of our friends continue working in the mission field in different parts of the world. Feel free to contact them or look in on what they're doing at www.citatoday.com

Jeff Pessina continues the work in The Philippines at Philippine Frontline Ministry – you can contact Jeff at jeff@thefrontline.asia or www.thefrontline.asia

You can view and read about a partial gallery of past members at Christ is the Answer Family on Facebook.

I am currently on the pastoral staff of a fabulous church in northeast Wisconsin, www.celebrationchurch.tv - we welcome your visit to this website and invite you to attend if you're ever in the area. You can also view our Sunday service live by simply clicking on the appropriate link. Pastor Mark (yes, my compadre in the '70s) is now senior pastor at Celebration and a well-known relationships speaker throughout the U.S. Check out his ministry at www.laughyourway.com (Laugh Your Way to a Better Marriage)

About the Author

Joe Grier has been involved in ministry since 1970 - music, missions, evangelism, pastor, teacher. He currently lives in Appleton, Wisconsin with Gayle and is on the pastoral staff at Celebration Church.

Check out Joe's blog at:
http://joehuffandpuff.blogspot.com/

Facebook: http://www.facebook.com/joe.grier.37

Twitter: http://twitter.com/@JoJoDF1

79798286R00136

Made in the USA
Lexington, KY
29 January 2018